TRENDS PERFECT
HOME

TRENDS PERFECT HOME

FOG CITY PRESS

Trends *Perfect Home* is produced in association with Trends Publishing International, 49 Main Highway, Ellerslie, Auckland, New Zealand

www.trendsideas.com

Publisher: David Johnson
Editorial Director: Paul Taylor
Trends Home Series Editor: Rachel Galyer
Associate Editor: Kelli Robson
Production Director: Louise Messer
Editorial Administrator: Kate Ballinger

Published by Fog City Press, 814 Montgomery Street, San Francisco, CA 94133 USA

Chief Executive Officer: John Owen
President: Terry Newell
Publisher: Lynn Humphries
Managing Editor: Janine Flew
Design Manager: Helen Perks
Editorial Coordinator: Kiren Thandi
Production Manager: Caroline Webber
Production Coordinator: James Blackman
Sales Manager: Emily Jahn
Vice President International Sales: Stuart Laurence

Series Design Concept: John Bull
Project Designer: Sally Browne
Text: Julia Richardson

ISBN 1 877019 14 3

Color reproduction by SC (Sang Choy) International Pte Ltd
Printed by LeeFung-Asco Printers
Printed in China

A Weldon Owen Production

Cover photography
Back cover TOP LEFT Architect: Warren Hedgpeth, Hedgpeth Architects; Photographer: Tim Maloney. TOP RIGHT Interior Designer: Talla Skogmo, Gunkelmann Interior Design; Architect: Kelly Davis. BOTTOM LEFT Interior Design: Dana Lane, Candlewick; Photographer: Shania Shegedyn. BOTTOM RIGHT Architect: S2F; Photographer: Shania Shegedyn.
Spine Interior Design: Mason Cowle, Suzie Wiley, Planit Architecture & Management; Photographer: David Sandison.
Front cover TOP LEFT Architect: Peter Lee, JPL Architectural Partnership; Photographer: Peter Mealin. TOP RIGHT Landscape Designer: Trudy Crerar, Natural Habitats; Architect: Andrew Patterson, Architects Patterson & Co; Photographer: Anton Curley. BOTTOM LEFT Designer: Darryl Gordon Design: Photographer: Simon Kenny. BOTTOM RIGHT Interior Designer: Margot Cordony; Photographer; Simon Kenny.

CONTENTS

INTRODUCTION

In the 21st century, the worlds of commerce and industry are
more homogenized, more demanding and more impersonal than
ever they were. Our homes provide the balance, offering us
the opportunity to surround ourselves with the sounds, shapes,
colors, objects and memories that delight us and that meet our
needs in a very personal way.

NEEDS, WANTS AND DESIRES

The contemporary home embodies two enormously valuable potentials: those of sanctuary and self expression. The kinds of environments that evoke those feelings differ from person to person. A pocket-sized city apartment with walls covered in framed photographs and a balcony thick with potplants might bring unspeakable joy to one person. For another, an avant-garde cube faced with sheer glass on one side, poised atop a cliff and furnished with austere modern designs, might be the most inspiring environment imaginable.

Intuition ought to tell us which surroundings are most likely to give us comfort, delight, peace and stimulation, but the fact is that many of us find our instincts clouded. There are so many possibilties that many of us have trouble deciding what truly gives us pleasure and what we really need.

Despite the overwhelming range of options, our personal instincts survive; we just need to rediscover them. One of the easiest and most effective strategies is to keep a diary of what goes on in the house for at least a couple of months, or up to a year, before a design or decorating project commences. Keep it simple; no deep reflections, just the facts. Such a journal can make you aware of habits and rituals so fundamental to your way of life that you could be astounded you had never recognized them before. It could record, for example, that the car always ends up parked on the street because the garage is in permanent use as a work shed. Or that the view from the spare bedroom of blossom trees in spring is heartbreakingly

A conservatory is neither a standard inclusion in a modern home, nor the kind of room you'd expect in the floorplan of a project home. Yet this simple space — plainly furnished, thick with greenery and deliciously musty with the smell of earth — is an unadulterated pleasure for its owners.

beautiful, but rarely glimpsed. Or that the newspapers put aside for recycling all but block the back door by the end of the week. Such observations could influence you to build a new garage, or relocate the master bedroom to a smaller room with a better outlook, or incorporate a storage bay for recycling somewhere.

People tend to be more confident about their aesthetic preferences than their architectural needs, but it is easy to be overwhelmed by the flood of commercialized trends, looks and products ingeniously and specifically devised to manipulate the individual's choosing power. A simple way of reconnecting with your intuitive likes and dislikes is to find some magazines or decorating books and tear out or tag the images to which you respond. Try to distinguish between those with simple visual appeal and those that you feel a genuine urge to occupy. After a while, a pattern should emerge, revealing a coherent set of colors, patterns, styles and textures that can serve as a launching pad for your projects.

DISCOVERY AND DIVERSITY

Almost anyone searching for a new home, remodeling an existing one or even reworking a single room is doing so in search of two things: space and light. These elements may embody the individual's need for personal space, a place which is the very antithesis of the modern work environment, or they may represent a human craving for a naturally healthy environment. It's a mistake, though, to assume that pursuing maximum space and light via architectural means will fulfill these desires. In the late 1980s and early 1990s, when a group of affluent home owners began to repopulate inner-urban areas of major cities, many 19th-century houses were gutted to create

❶

❶ Eclectic collections are most likely to succeed when every element is linked by a common theme. This could be a consistent color, period or pattern, but by far the most unifying element is a sense of passion. Choose pieces because you love them on their own merits, regardless of style or provenance, and a prevailing aesthetic will emerge naturally.

❷ A broad expanse of glazing, an all-white interior and smart but unfussy furnishings allow the glorious water view to become the focus of this room.

❸ A subdued palette and an uncomplicated sense of symmetry evoke the desired mood of composure and calm in this modern bedroom.

❷

❸

open spaces as vast and as well lit as the architectural shell allowed. The motivation was understandable, but the result was often disappointing. Rather than achieving a sense of spaciousness, the act of replacing a number of small rooms with a single, albeit expansive, four-walled space often made the house feel more limited. Fully exposed from the moment anyone passed through the front door, the interior presented no diversity, no opportunity for intimacy, no passing visual delights. Removing the internal walls also meant losing some of the traditional floorplan's inherent dynamics, its ability to shift from one purpose or one mood to the next. The lesson learned was that it may not be sheer physical space that makes a home feel large, but the incorporation of a variety of spaces.

That's not to say that a room of soaring proportions isn't an uplifting space to occupy. Far from it. Grand dimensions can make for breathtaking interiors, but floor area alone isn't what makes a home pleasurable. More important than sheer space is á sense of animation. A house or apartment that is active, that involves movement, changes of pace, altering views and different experiences, is more than a mere shelter, it's a home.

STIMULATION AND CHOICE

An interior can be invested with energy in many ways, perhaps the most influential of which is color. A paint-box approach, where each room takes a different hue — a daffodil bedroom, a sky blue kitchen, a tulip pink dining room, a bud green home office — is a cheerful but unsubtle manipulation of the senses, but even when an entire house is furnished with a

Stepping into this bedroom is like entering another world, far away from the bustle of the household. More than the size, shape or position of the room, it's the languorous shade of blue on the walls that makes this space so serene.

consistent palette, deftly handled accents of color can be used to signal shifts from one space to the next. For example, a chic urban cottage might be decorated throughout in smooth shades of cream and cocoa. In the living room, those tones might feature on the walls, carpet and sofa, but blue accents — dove blue feature stitching on the drapes, blue cushions, a blue glazed vase and a pair of blue armchairs — will give this room a fresh and free-spirited character. In the kitchen, the basic tones could be strengthened by chocolate-toned joinery. In the bedroom, they might team with lavender cushions and drapes for a gently feminine mood. In a teenager's bedroom, the color accents might be provided by denim bed linen and a denim beanbag. In small but persuasive ways, these minimal color shifts evoke whole new worlds of sensation, extracting from a given architectural shell a universe of varied and purposeful character.

The same effect might be achieved using any number of different design tools — orientation, texture, lighting, acoustics — alone or in combination. Positioning family living rooms on sunny walls creates spaces that are awash with healthy sunshine for the greater part of the day, making them a perfect place in which children can play or adults relax with the newspaper. Constructing the floorplan so that an adult's bedroom is removed from the main activity areas — on a second floor, say, or at the end of a long hallway — reinforces the notion that it is a place to be visited purposefully by those who sleep there and not by any family member looking for a place to watch TV or for some clothes to borrow.

❶

❶ Voluminous interiors are in vogue, but sometimes a small and cozy room can be a more pleasurable space to occupy. This is particularly true of bedrooms, where more compact dimensions tend to create more invitingly intimate spaces.

❷ Hallways are often treated as dull, functional spaces, yet they can contribute much to the sense of animation in a house.

This cool, white passage adds a sense of the dynamic to a conventional period home.

❸ Exposed steel beams and furnishings with a cheerfully industrial air make this a stimulating environment for a home office. At the end of the day, however, a change in lighting plays up the warmth of the wooden wall panels and this busy work space becomes a welcoming space in which to unwind.

❷

❸

Cladding a family room in sea-grass flooring and wash-and-wear acrylic paint, then furnishing it with casual wicker sofas topped with big, washable cushions clearly defines its role as the one place in the house where the noise and mess of rambunctious activity are sanctioned. Wrapping another room in sumptuous carpet and textured wall finishes and filling it with deliciously plump armchairs and ottomans marks it out as a space for quiet, sensual, slow living, especially late at night. The juxtaposition of two spaces so differently and so lucidly defined in terms of character and purpose imbues even the tiniest of cottages with invigorating energy simply by presenting alternatives, opportunities within a single house for experiences of a different pitch, tempo or tone.

A century ago, science fiction writers tended to visualize a future of uniform, modular, synthetic habitats. Instead, we crave spaces that express our individual personalities. We search out eccentric flea market finds or one-off, top-end designs, we look for ways to modify floorplans to suit the habits of our particular household, we deliberate between shades of taupe and ecru and stone and we muse over what to display and what to conceal behind closed doors. If our motivations are superficial then we gain nothing for our efforts, but if our aim is to craft a space that truly defines our lives and our values, then our reward is surroundings that are rich in character. Such a home has the power to counter the sense of isolation felt by many in our society, to shelter and comfort the household, catching the imagination of all who enter. Such a home will become a treasury of meaning and memory.

A faded rug, a butcher's block worn down by use and time, a collection of childrens' paintings and a colorful assortment of kitchen accessories give this room a distinctive character that has clearly evolved naturally around its occupants.

perfect

ENTRANCES

Functionally and aesthetically, an entrance is a starting point. It is also the public face of a private domain, a chance to make a clear declaration of personal style to the world at large. Perhaps most importantly, it is a zone of welcome, a physical space that should greet visitors with cheer, but also embrace every member of the household with a sense of warmth and security on a daily basis.

PERFECT ENTRANCES

The front door to your house is more than an aperture; it's a zone. The area immediately before and immediately after it forms a pocket of space in which you — and your guests — leave behind a public world and enter an intimate domain. Aesthetically, it sets the tone for the interior, but it also sets the stage for a personal transition from the public you to the private you. It should be a pick-me-up, a space where the "real" you is welcomed and made comfortable.

An entranceway must also provide privacy to those already inside the house and, ideally, shelter to those entering it. Overhanging eaves or an external awning will offer protection from harsh sunshine and rain. Inevitably the flooring just inside the front door will suffer from wear as remnants of grit and grime from the street grind down the surface. Consider using a material more commonly used externally. A mosaic of pebbles could be laid in a small foyer or a series of pavers set like stepping stones into a wood-floored hallway.

PREVIOUS PAGES Dynamic entrances are those that evoke a sense of passage or of transition between worlds, such as this long, low-ceilinged, glass-lined hallway (left) or this unusual foyer comprising a pond and a wooden bridge (right).

❶ Because an entry hall is merely a passageway, not a destination, purposeful furniture arrangements are unnecessary. Instead, use this space to feature idiosyncratic pieces that have no particular role except, perhaps, to display favorite collectibles and keepsakes.

❷ A table in a foyer will be used only occasionally. It can, therefore, house pieces too precious or fragile for regular use.

❸ This Mediterranean-inspired house is built around a central court-yard. The wrought-iron entrance gates open onto a cloistered area that leads off into the interior of the house and on to the paved area around the pond.

DOORS AND ENTRANCEWAYS

On a functional level, a front door must offer privacy and security. Once those requirements have been met, however, you can afford to get creative. This is, after all, your public face, the feature that gives visitors and passersby their first impression of the house and its occupants.

You can make a big statement with the front door without having to maintain that pitch throughout the rest of the house. The front door's singularity of purpose gives it an independence from all the other rooms of the house, allowing you the freedom to do something quite different. Some sort of stylistic link should remain, however. For example, an outsized door clad in copper with a spiraling copper handle might give way to an interior of quirky modern design. A door of sandblasted glass might lead into a house with a cool, clean, industrial aesthetic. A red lacquer door might open onto a house where an all-white interior is interrupted sparingly and dramatically with accents of scarlet in the form of a painting, a single armchair or a scattering of cushions.

If you're not in a position to have a door custom made or if you are obliged to take a conservative approach in the interest of preserving the character of an area or a development, you still have the option of personalizing your entrance in a more modest way. Something as simple as a potted plant or a garden chair can be used to give your entrance some character.

❶ A very traditional doorway featuring panels of decorative glass sets the tone for an authentically furnished period house. The surrounding glass panels on both the rear and the front doors increase the amount of light penetrating the interior, greatly improving the ambiance of the central corridor.

❶

❷ Double doors of luminous frosted glass panels make the most of the available daylight to illuminate the entry foyer, but still offer a degree of privacy.

❷

FOYERS AND ENTRY HALLS

In some houses, the sense of transition is aided by an entrance hall or foyer. Essentially it serves as a holding place in which residents or visitors can literally rid themselves of the trappings of the outside world — coats, umbrellas, car keys — before proceeding into the body of the house. It makes sense, then, that this space should be furnished for that purpose, with a coat rack or coat pegs, an umbrella stand and a small thin table where keys, mail, a handbag and so on can be deposited. Naturally enough, this hall table can also be the repository of things that need grabbing on the way out: a shopping list, library books, school bags — anything that's easily forgotten in the haste of flight.

A particularly spacious foyer is an excellent spot for a small workstation, in which case a comfortable chair, a telephone and a petite desk or table that offers some storage space for writing materials and documents should be included. This kind of set-up is suitable for anyone managing the affairs of the household, but is inadequate for a genuine home office.

❶ A slim hall table is a sensible inclusion in a foyer, providing a spot for keys, mail or mobile phones to be deposited on entering the house. A display of family photographs or treasured collectibles will give the piece a decorative as well as a functional role.

❶

❷ An intricate paneled door and ornate floor insets are an impressive introduction to the interior of this palatial art deco home.

❸ Cluttered with beloved treasures of all kinds, this foyer conveys a distinct impression of its owner's personality.

❹ This pebble mosaic is an exotic treatment for an interior floor, conjuring visions of moody villas in southern Europe and northern Africa. It is also surprisingly practical, offering a rugged surface that will be little affected by the heavy traffic around an entry door.

❺ The lowest level of this small entrance is lined with exterior pavers that will stand up to heavy wear and tear.

❶ In this entrance hall, large stone pavers have been set into the wooden flooring in an orderly, geometric grid. The effect is smart and arresting and sets the tone for an aesthetically stimulating interior, but the installation also has a practical purpose. The extra-durable pavers withstand the worst of the grit that is walked through from the street into the house, protecting the more delicate wooden surface of the interior from damage.

❷ Petite apartment foyers can be made to feel more spacious by lining one wall with mirrors. This approach immediately eliminates the sense of enclosure, but can result in distracting or irritating reflections. A carefully positioned artwork can avoid the possibility of unwelcome reflections, without reducing the sense of openness achieved by the mirrors.

❸ Entry foyers are often small rooms that do not have the benefit of external windows to furnish them with a source of natural light. Installing a skylight or lining the entire ceiling with translucent panels can flood the area with sunlight, making it a far more welcoming space.

❶

2

LIVING ROOMS

Relaxation comes in different forms for different people. For one
person, it could be enjoying a drink with friends; for another,
it could be curling up with a book; yet another may prefer lying
on the floor with kids and their toys. The living room is the space
charged with accommodating these diverse activities. It must,
therefore, be able to undergo a role change at a moment's notice.

PERFECT LIVING ROOMS

A living room is not a work space, unlike a kitchen or a home office or even a bathroom, yet it has more diverse demands placed upon it than any other room in the house. It is the most public of domestic spaces, yet it must also have a warmth and intimacy to soothe and comfort the individual. It is the venue for parties, social gatherings and entertainments of various kinds, but it is also a place for solitude and retreat.

Devising a room to fulfill these many roles is a challenge indeed. The temptation, of course, is to opt for neutrality in the hope that, by virtue of its indifferent character, the room will not prove markedly unsuitable for any occasion. This isn't a bad strategy, but it is a negative one, and one that robs you of an opportunity for self-expression. If personal preferences — whether quirky or classic, hi-tech or old-world, rustic or refined — are permitted to influence and inform the style

PREVIOUS PAGES A comfortable place to sit is the one essential of the living room. Almost as important is a focal point. A collection of framed prints and artifacts is a simple way of giving a room a very personal showpiece, but in a house blessed with a view, the vista alone can take center stage.

❶ In this ultra-stylish space, modern pieces of furniture are teamed with design classics, such as the Alvar Aalto side table. Even the television has a distinguished quality to it. To maintain this pared-back look, less attractive equipment, including a stereo and a DVD player, is installed in a half-height wall and attached to the television by concealed wires.

❶

❶ The grand tone of this space, designed as a formal living room, and of a neighboring formal dining room was established by the installation of ceilings set 12 inches (30 cm) higher than those in the more private areas of the house.

❷ Hardy terrazzo floors overlaid with super-tough sea-grass matting and finished off with smart, but casual, wicker furniture are well suited to this relaxed family living area.

❷

of the living room, the result will be a space that succeeds on both a public and a private level. Nothing makes people less comfortable — consciously or otherwise — than pretence. A very personal living space has a recognizable integrity to it and as long as it has been executed with confidence, it is more than likely to put visitors at ease and engage them with its passions and its peculiarities. And while there is a case to be made that a neutral and deliberately unstimulating space can be a calming environment, it's also true that a reconfirmation of our identity and our differences can be a valuable tonic for the individual in a society of homogenized consumerism.

❸ Tiling the floor of a living room that opens onto an outdoor area is a practical tactic, given that the hard surface should be able to withstand the wear and tear caused by the grit, mud and dust that is walked in from the garden.

❸

① ❶ Identifying the household's favorite modes of relaxation and recreation and making room for them in the floorplan is a sure way of creating a successful living space. In this house, where the occupants love to entertain, the installation of a bar wasn't a luxury but a necessity.

❷ Open-plan areas encourage a natural drift from the dining table to the lounge, a bonus in a house where the owners entertain frequently.

②

③

❸ Living rooms tend to attract plenty of clutter, from school bags and sports gear to old magazines and craft baskets. A bank of built-in cabinetry ensures that these items can be cleared away in a matter of minutes.

❹ A symmetrical layout immediately imbues a space with formality. In this case, it also draws attention to an antique chaise longue and an elegant period mantel.

④

SEATING

Of all the furniture items in the house, only a mattress has a closer relationship with the body than the seating in the living room. For that reason, lounges, armchairs and other forms of seating must offer comfort and support. Take your time over this purchase, spending at least 15 minutes sitting and considering the firmness of the seat cushion, the height of the back and arm supports and the depth of the seat. Short and tall people can have quite disparate needs when it comes to seating. If there is a variety of heights in your household, a selection of different armchairs might be the best solution.

Seating will also be subject to considerable wear and tear over time, so it makes sense to spend as much as the budget will allow to get a better piece, prioritizing your expenditure here rather than on purchases of items such as storage pieces or decorative accessories. High-quality lounges and armchairs have hardwood frames and a sprung base, a construction that will prove robust for a decade or more. Those with softwood frames often start to fall apart after as little as three or four years. Feather cushions are considered a luxury and indeed they are sumptuously soft, but they do flatten under body

Lounges without arms have a sleek, modern look. They're also great for entertaining, with a number of guests able to line up along the seat, facing in various directions to be part of different conversations. They're not as good for casual use by a family or a couple, because they provide no end pieces for cozy tandem slouching. Instead, they're likely to be used by a single person who will take full advantage of the lounge's length by lying flat out.

weight and need daily, if not hourly, plumping to preserve their springy good looks. Foam and polyester cushions are more common among less expensive lounges and armchairs. A pragmatic compromise, both in terms of expense and style, is the feather-wrapped foam cushion, which has some of the long-lasting buoyancy of foam with the plush feel of feathers.

When buying a lounge or armchair, always take up the supplier's offer of a stain-resistant treatment. Better yet, ask to have the piece made up in a base cloth, such as canvas, and have your chosen fabric sewn up into removable covers so that they can be taken off and cleaned regularly. The popularity of the so-called shabby chic look has given some people the impression that a removable cover is necessarily a voguishly shaggy cover with a loose fit. This is not so: some quite tailored looks and tight fits can be achieved with a removable cover. Opting for a removable cover generally adds to the expense of the lounge or armchair but it could conceivably double or triple the life of the piece. It also gives you the freedom to change the look of the room with a new set of covers either seasonally or when updating the style of the whole room, without having to pay for a complete new furniture suite.

❶ Including a number of armchairs in a living room has two advantages. It makes it possible to cater for the ergonomic requirements of different-sized members of the household and it can aid the comfort of guests, who often appreciate some private space.

❶

❷ Leather upholstery is a marvelous choice in the living room. It can look masterly and traditional or sharp and modern, and the surface easily withstands the food spills and grubby hands of guests of all ages.

❸ An upright armchair can be used almost as a piece of sculpture, introducing a particular aesthetic note into the living room.

❹ This cozy area includes a variety of seating options: a lounge for lolling, an armchair for personal relaxation and a window seat for a sunlit morning with the paper.

❺ Modular lounges facilitate sitting, lounging, sleeping and perching and can be reconfigured to suit a different room or aspect.

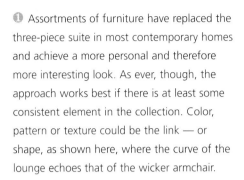

❶ Assortments of furniture have replaced the three-piece suite in most contemporary homes and achieve a more personal and therefore more interesting look. As ever, though, the approach works best if there is at least some consistent element in the collection. Color, pattern or texture could be the link — or shape, as shown here, where the curve of the lounge echoes that of the wicker armchair.

❷ An arrangement of wingback armchairs and double-ended chaise longues provides an unusual variety of seats and seating positions, making this formal living room a particularly successful space for social occasions.

❸ It was always intended that the view should take center stage in this relaxed living area. Accordingly, neutral colors were used on the walls and floor and for the upholstery. A scattering of cushions picks up on the naturally vibrant palette of the ocean-front terrain just beyond the balcony.

❶ The muted earth tones of this stylishly casual living room
reflect the surrounding desert environment of an adobe-style
house. An arrangement that includes a modular lounge,
a pair of armchairs and an ottoman forms a relaxed social
circle, while two chaise longues provide a romantic setting
for long nights by the fireside.

❷ This living space bears the influence of the owners' love of Indonesian interiors. In a hot climate, upholstered wooden lounges achieve a relaxed but sophisticated feeling without the heavy-set look of conventional fully upholstered suites.

❸ In cooler climates, layers of soft furnishings convey an impression of comfort and warmth. Here, plush flooring, floor-length drapes and cushion-scattered lounges create an enticingly snug interior.

❹ Always an expensive option, leather lounges justify their cost by outlasting most upholstered pieces. Scissors, knives and puppy teeth may harm them, but splashes of wine and splodges of food will not.

❶

❶ This living area is part of an open-plan space that also incorporates a dining area and a kitchen. The openness of the floorplan allows maximum interaction with the tree-enclosed setting of the house, visible through a long line of sliding, wood-framed glass doors. Aligning the lounges so that they define a smaller pocket of space achieves the intimacy that all living areas require, whether or not they are part of an open-plan room.

❷ In this warmly neutral room of barley-colored walls and stone flooring, an oversized custom-built lounge is as much a showpiece as the paintings of artist Paul Critchley.

❷

FOCAL POINTS

Most rooms in the house have a clear purpose. The bedroom is primarily for rest, the kitchen for cooking, the bathroom for bathing, the office for work and so on. Consequently, each of these rooms has a natural focal point: the bed in the bedroom, the range in the kitchen, the tub in the bathroom and the desk in the office. This feature is the starting point for furniture placement, color schemes and decorating ideas.

The living room, however, is not a space that can be so easily defined by its function. Its focal point, therefore, is a feature that must be consciously selected and installed. Without an element that draws focus and sets the tone, the space will seem lightweight, characterless, purposeless, even amateurish. Moreover, unless you nominate a centerpiece for your living room, you will probably find that the television becomes the focal point of the space by default.

The focus of the living room might be something that fulfills a practical function — an antique armchair, a vintage lamp, or a suede-covered ottoman large enough to serve as chaise longue or coffee table as the occasion requires — but it can also be something entirely decorative. This is definitely the place for a stimulating work of art or a cascading display of framed

An extravagantly sized mirror draws attention to the classically styled mantel below. A large bowl with sculptural qualities completes this spectacular composition.

family photographs. It could be that a collection of kitsch salt and pepper shakers, Venetian glass or battered old shoe lasts becomes the room's showpiece. It might be a model boat that took a lifetime to build, a treasury of children's books with picturesque hardcovers, an heirloom family quilt hung on the wall, or a Scandinavian rug spread out on the floor. It's easy to see how any one of these examples could be used as a focal point and to recognize how its presence might establish the tone of the space, serve as a starting point for all other style choices and act as a strong expression of the character of the household and its inhabitants.

Traditionally — before video games and televisions, even before radios — the hearth was the focus of every living space. Today, it is still a beloved feature in living rooms the world over, even in areas where the climate is relatively mild. True, the fireplace generates heat, but its amber glow, its crackles, spits and smoky smells provide sensory delights on many different levels. When not in use, however, the fireplace is a dead zone and, as such, is a very desolate sort of centerpiece for the room. If in winter your living room clusters around a lively hearth, you might consider rearranging the furniture come spring so that a large window with a garden view or an antique table that houses an assortment of collectible ceramics becomes the space's character-defining feature. An alternative is to fill the empty hearth in some way that recalls those heart-warming flames, but without giving off any real heat. A series of candles, perhaps set into a bed of small pebbles, is one way of filling the void. Another option is a small pile of twig balls, each one illuminated by a small, battery-operated set of fairy lights.

❶ A quirky, contemporary collection that comprises candle holders, distinctive ceramics and a framed painting invest this mantel with interest and intrigue even when there is no fire in the hearth.

❶

❷ A dramatic, recessed fireplace enhanced by a strategically poised sconce light is a strong focal point in this living room. In months when there is no need for an open fire, the long, sleek slot windows that emphasize the room's impressive dimensions are the most dominant visual element. ❷

❶ When not in use, this modest hearth is completely dominated by the vast slabs of garden view framed by enormous areas of fixed-pane glazing and folding doors. As soon as it is filled with flames, however, it immediately captures the attention of everyone in the room.

❷ No shop-bought centerpiece could challenge the ever-lasting appeal of a water view. This living space succumbs to the lure of the seaside, with walls of glazing and a circular arrangement of furniture that allows almost everyone a glimpse of the water.

❸ This space proves that the idea of a themed room does not have to be repellently gimmicky. In this house by the sea, a marine theme is subtly executed in the living area. A moody portrait of a fish and a nostalgic model yacht are all it takes to allude to the ocean-front location.

❶

STORAGE

There is much to stash away in a living room. For a start, very few modern living areas do not contain some form of audiovisual equipment. Then, of course, there are books, games, videos, CDs, children's toys, musical instruments, school bags, perhaps items used in sewing or craft, magazines, family photos and so on. There are basically two approaches to storage: concealment or display. Those who prefer the former will tend toward entertainment centers where television and stereo can be hidden behind closed doors, coffee tables that incorporate storage drawers and ottomans with hinged tops that can hide old magazines or balls of wool. Those who opt for display will go for lots of open shelving where the spines of hundreds of CDs or DVDs can be seen at a glance.

❶ Attempting to conceal the presence of massive screens and towering speakers is a monumental challenge. Often the best option is to leave them on display in a purpose-built cabinet that at least keeps them from trailing skeins of electrical cables across the floor.

❷ The question of which items are fit for display and which are not can only be answered by the individual. Many a music lover would agree that there is nothing more appealing than the sight of hundreds of CDs.

❸ Artful wood storage is a practical companion to the hearth, a graphic and textural part of the room's design and a clever way of reducing the impact of the television.

Whatever mode you favor, the fact remains that adequate storage space is essential in a living room. The flexibility of the space relies on its capacity to spill over with paraphernalia for one kind of pursuit — such as the games, controls and cords of a video game — then swallow them up to make way for the next, entirely different activity, such as entertaining a visitor. Even something as simple as the inclusion of a toy box can go a long way toward freeing up the living room and maximizing its potential. Providing a place where dolls, trucks, building blocks and board games can be stashed away means that the room can easily undergo the transformation from crèche and playroom through the daylight hours into a place where adults can seek some restorative peace and quiet at night.

❷

❸

❶ A row of shelving installed below an internal window is a visually low-key way of providing a substantial amount of storage space in this casual living area.

❷ In period houses, the spaces to either side of the chimney breast are often wasted. Installing custom-built cabinetry that recalls the original style of the house is an attractive, practical solution.

❸ Displaying this pretty china on open shelves obviously takes up more space than stacking the pieces and stashing them in a cabinet. It does, however, contribute enormously to the character of the room.

❶

❶ In this rambling living room, a stately wooden cabinet conceals audio-visual equipment, ensuring that the broad hearth retains focus. A drawer below the cabinet doors is a simple but very useful inclusion, providing storage for the inevitable accumulation of video tapes, DVDs and CDs.

❷ A blank television screen — particularly a very big, blank television screen bracketed by audio speakers and various other electrical components — is an unattractive element in any living space. Here, frosted glass doors screen the audiovisual gear while exposing the contents of the display shelves on either side. When the equipment is in use, the doors slide across to cover the shelves, forming a rather handsome, luminous frame for the screen.

❷

3

KITCHENS

The kitchen is the hardest-working space in the home, the place where hot pans and hunger collide. It is also the site of all the unscheduled interactions and encounters that are the essence of family life. If the functional needs of the kitchen are addressed, its social role will follow. A kitchen that performs well will be well used and well loved.

PERFECT KITCHENS

The contemporary kitchen is a place where the whole family gathers to work and play, sometimes around the focus of a meal, but just as often in those unplanned interactions that take place over a cup of coffee, at the end of the day or as the dishes are being cleared after dinner. The potential for social activity is, however, undermined unless the functional role of the kitchen is addressed effectively and efficiently.

A well-designed kitchen must have the sound planning of a work site. Appliances should fulfill the demands required of them and be of the best quality possible within a given budget. They should also be positioned so that they can be used safely. If, for example, the kitchen door is located between the range

❷

❸

PREVIOUS PAGES Sleek and streamlined or generously open to view, all kitchens are governed by a need for safe, accessible and durable work areas.

❶ Comprehensively furnished with quality appliances, this high-performance kitchen still manages to retain a cheerful warmth. The blushing pink highlights, an eccentric approach to decorating, and the inclusion of a broad island that also serves as an eating place guarantee a warm welcome to all.

❷ Installing sinks and a stovetop in this counter ensures that the cook is always part of the action in the adjacent living area.

❸ Including a casual eating area in the floorplan encourages visitors and helpers into the kitchen.

and the sink, then the possibility of a collision between a cook carrying a hot and heavy pan and another family member is all too likely. And all the appliances, along with the work surfaces where food preparation takes place, must be well lit to minimize the risk of accidents.

Storage must not only be of adequate capacity, but be arranged so that the kitchen can be used efficiently and effectively. Having to travel long distances from where the kettle is located to the cabinet that contains tea or coffee is a waste of time and can make a kitchen very inconvenient to use over the long term.

Wall, counter and floor surfaces must also be a match for the tough working conditions of the kitchen. They will be subject to heavy wear and tear and will also be exposed to heat, moisture and grease. Surfaces that perform badly in such an environment soon become an eyesore or even a safety risk.

In most cases, kitchens require more planning time and more money than any other room in the house. The need for high-quality surfaces and fixtures and high-performance appliances makes that an unavoidable necessity. If, however, the room's functional requirements are met, there is no reason why a kitchen can't be built to last a generation or more.

❶ Kitchen sinks are commonly placed under windows for very practical reasons. Light coming in through the window illuminates what is essentially a work area, while the view — as modest as it may be — is far preferable to the oppressive facade of a solid wall.

❶

| ❷ | ❸ |
| ❹ | ❺ |

❷ This room deftly serves two roles, one as a well-appointed kitchen, the other as a casual living area for a young family. Floor-to-ceiling glass door panels and extensive ceiling glazing supply a generous volume of natural light.

❸ Corners can prove difficult in a kitchen floorplan. The angle is often too awkward for good storage, but a cooktop, installed on the diagonal, makes efficient use of the space.

❹ In a small kitchen, look to the walls for extra storage. A few open shelves can free up cabinet space and improve accessibility.

❺ Equipped with a sink, a microwave oven and storage baskets for fresh vegetables, this island functions as an independent work zone in a busy kitchen.

①

②

❶ Most of the storage in this peninsula counter is accessible from the kitchen side of the cabinetry, but two drawers face the living area, providing a neat storage solution for phone books, note pads and pens.

❷ The space between the top of wall cabinets and the ceiling is often left vacant, but, as this kitchen shows, filling the void with cabinetry is an easy way of maximizing your storage capacity.

❸ Designing the storage component of this sleek island so that it looks like a freestanding sideboard gives a tailored, furnished look to the outer face of an open-plan kitchen.

③

WORK ZONES

Since the 1950s, kitchen floorplans have been designed with an eye to what is called the "work triangle." The work triangle links the three main activity centers of the room: the refrigerator, the sink and the range. The theory goes that the total distance around the triangle — from range to sink, sink to refrigerator, refrigerator to range — should be around 20 feet (7 m). Any more, and the cook would have to trudge long distances between one activity and the next; any less, and the cook would be too cramped.

The basic principle of the work triangle is sound and can be useful in the planning of a new kitchen, but it is not always easily applied in an existing kitchen. Rather than hold to the 20-foot (7-m) rule, just try to position those three main activity centers so that they are only a few steps apart from each other. If even that poses a problem, prioritize the locations of the sink and the range, since it is between these two sites that you will often need to work quickly, carrying heavy and usually hot pots and pans, and let the refrigerator take a less prominent position somewhere else in the room. Also, try to avoid having the kitchen door located within the triangle: such a configuration will force household traffic to cross the cook's path, a source of irritation for all involved.

The back wall of this kitchen, fitted with a double refrigerator and a double oven, is the zone where the serious cooking action takes place. With its ample countertops and its utility sink, the island can serve this primary work zone, or function as a separate unit where simple snacks can be prepared.

Increasingly, the concept of the work triangle is being replaced by the notion that a kitchen should be made up of multiple workstations. This more hybrid approach reflects some of the social changes made over the last half century. No longer is the mother of the household the chief occupant of the kitchen, being both cook and housemaid to the entire family. Instead, the kitchen might be used by several members of the family in the preparation of a single meal, or in the preparation of a number of different meals. It may also be the place where small children play or watch television, where older students do their homework, or where adults organize bill payments and correspondence — or it may frequently be the venue for impromptu social occasions.

The most common and perhaps most useful workstation is centered around an appliance garage, which holds a toaster, a kettle and the various bits and pieces required to make a simple breakfast or a quick snack. Positioning it close to the sink so that the kettle can be filled easily makes sense; providing it with its own separate sink makes it function that much more independently. Along similar lines, a workstation could be created by locating a refrigerator and a microwave oven close together and away from the main body of the kitchen so that school-age children can cater for themselves and their friends without interrupting the preparation of the family meal. A serious cook's kitchen might include a baking area with 30-inch (76-cm) high marble counters suitable for the kneading and rolling of pastry located close to the oven. An entertainer's kitchen could feature an under-counter bar fridge, stocked only with beverages, located on the periphery of the kitchen along with cupboards for glass storage, a second sink and perhaps even a half-width dishwasher. The specific elements and the location of workstations depend entirely on the kitchen and those using it.

❶ Hanging pot storage above the range helps to contain the activity of the cook, enabling other areas to function without obstruction, even while a hot meal is being prepared.

❷ In this modern country kitchen, the sink and the range are located within easy reach of each other, yet with plenty of countertop space for food preparation in between.

❶

❷

❸ Pull-out cutting boards are installed in every unit of cabinetry throughout this kitchen, just below the top drawer. The extra surface area makes it possible for many cooks to work at once. ❸

❷

❸

❶ One edge of this island serves the oven and refrigerator at the far end of the kitchen, while another faces the cooktop.

❷ Positioned on the corner of the island, the sink can be part of cooking activities focused around the cooktop or can simply be used by anyone grabbing a snack and a drink from the nearby refrigerator.

❸ A steel-topped island fitted with a utility sink and a cutting board serves a purely functional role. Next to it, a wood-topped counter provides a warmer surface that can be used either for food preparation or as a casual eating area.

Eating zones

The provision of some sort of table space goes a long way toward turning a kitchen into a multifunctional, communal room. It becomes the site for casual meals, but it can also be used as a place for adults to read through the day's mail while a pot reaches the boil, where a teenager can sit and talk about the day as a parent washes and chops vegetables for dinner or where a young child can sit with paper and crayons under the watchful eye of the cook.

Open-plan kitchens that specifically incorporate living and dining spaces are obviously designed to encourage this sort of intermingling, but it can also be facilitated in self-contained kitchens. Generously proportioned rooms can be graced with a welcoming, freestanding table, while even the tiniest of kitchens can usually squeeze in a drop-down table fixed to a wall.

Eating zones can be incorporated into the fitted cabinetry of a kitchen. The most basic strategy is simply to extend the depth or the length of a countertop. Extending the countertop beyond a run of cabinetry and supporting the overhang with legs forms a table-like arrangement with room for stools underneath. Alternatively, topping an island or peninsula of standard 24-inch (61-cm) deep cabinets with a counter that is 30 to 36 inches (76 to 92 cm) deep creates an overhang that can function as an eating area. A short overhang might be self-supporting but a deeper one may require supporting legs. A common variation is to fix a raised counter at the outer edge of the island or peninsula. The change in height between the main counter and the breakfast bar counter makes it clear where the activity and paraphernalia of one zone should end and the other begin. It also acts as a screen, shielding the often untidy work surface from view.

❶ A switch in materials helps distinguish between the area of the counter that serves as a work surface and that which forms a small breakfast bar.

❶

❷ | ❸
❹ | ❺

❷ Access to the last unit in a row of cabinets is always slightly hindered by the proximity of the wall. In this kitchen, the decision was made to take advantage of that limitation by installing a slim countertop from one end unit to another on the facing wall. The cabinets can still be used for storage, but obviously only for items that are needed infrequently.

❸ A small island with a shallow overhang forms the simplest of eating areas.

❹ A circular countertop at the end of an island creates a bistro-style eating area.

❺ A vast slab of granite supplies an overhang on two sides of this island, making room for four diners without impinging on the food-preparation area.

❶ Not every kitchen needs a full-scale dining space, but installing even a slim overhang and a few stools creates an area where friends can chat over a coffee or where children can work or play while a parent prepares the family meal.

❷ Integrated features, such as ranges and sinks, should be positioned to one end of a counter so that cooking tasks do not intrude on the eating zone.

❸ An L-shaped structure makes a clear distinction between the eating area and the work surfaces of this peninsula.

❹ Installed in an open-plan living area, this island has to be able to function as a work space as well as serve as the room's dining table. A slab of glass provides a hygienic and waterproof work surface but also gives the unit a sophisticated, furnished feel.

LIGHTING

The kitchen is essentially a work space, and like any work space it must be well lit if it is to function effectively and safely. A good and flexible kitchen lighting scheme contains both task lighting and ambient lighting.

Task lighting is all about providing adequate illumination in any of the areas where work takes place: the counters where food is prepared, the range where meals are cooked, the sink where dishes are washed and so on. Fixtures should be located so that they cast a bright, directional light onto work surfaces. Downlights or tracklights mounted on the ceiling or on the underside of wall-hung cabinets are ideal. Pendant lights can also be used, provided they are hung low over the relevant area. If they are hung too high, their light will be diffused and become too weak to serve as task lighting. Pendants should also be positioned away from the cooktop, because high temperatures can cause the shades to crack. Recessed downlights are perhaps the best of all options, as they sit flush with the ceiling and do not expose any dirt-attracting surface area. Surface-mounted downlights, tracklights and pendant lights

Ultra-sleek pendant lights shine brightly on the work areas around the sink. Recessed ceiling downlights furnish the room with background, ambient lighting.

all attract grease and dust in the hot and sticky environment of the kitchen and therefore require frequent cleaning.

Ambient lighting provides illumination at a less intense level, suitable for simple activities such as grabbing a juice from the refrigerator, arranging flowers in a vase, unpacking the shopping or chatting on the phone. A pendant light or two, installed in addition to the task lighting, can serve the purpose well. An alternative and more streamlined solution is to install a series of downlights in the ceiling, then assign them in banks to different switches so that the flick of one switch turns on the fixtures that function as task lighting above the work surfaces. The flick of a different switch activates just three or four lights, spaced evenly across the ceiling, that deliver adequate light levels for those less demanding tasks. If it is at all possible, have dimmers fitted to the lights. Used with dimmers, the fixtures installed as task lighting can do double duty as ambient lights. Dimming lights even slightly can also make a surprisingly big difference to energy consumption.

❶ Pendant lights attract more grease and dirt than recessed lights and therefore require more maintenance, but they also offer a greater potential for enhancing the character of the space. Here, steel domes reinforce the kitchen's sleek urbanity.

❷ This island serves as both a work area and an eating zone. Fitted with dimmers, these pendant lights can be adjusted to supply either strong task lighting or the more gentle illumination that suits a casual meal.

❸ Where ceilings are high, light from ceiling-mounted fittings can be too diffuse. Here, panels fixed over the top of the wall units bring the light sources closer to the counters.

❶

STORAGE

Good storage relies more on logic than on budget or available space. All the most frequently used items should be stored somewhere between eye level and hip height, making them easy to see and relatively easy to access. Storage below hip height should be reserved for such things as large oven trays, baking tins, surplus cutting boards and spare pot holders: items that are used infrequently and pose no danger to curious babies and toddlers. The highest cabinets are a good spot for more precious and fragile objects such as antique china, fine glassware and serving platters.

❶ Open storage is characteristic of country kitchens. Here, deep shelves on all sides of a hefty island give ready access to tableware, while making the most of the ceramics' cheerful designs and colorful glazes.

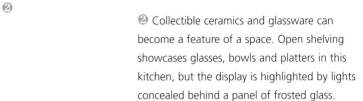

❷ Collectible ceramics and glassware can become a feature of a space. Open shelving showcases glasses, bowls and platters in this kitchen, but the display is highlighted by lights concealed behind a panel of frosted glass.

❸ A cabinet for the storage of tableware and servingware was built into the wall cavity of a pantry at one end of this kitchen. Faced with aluminum-framed glass doors, the cabinet supplies plenty of storage without disrupting the low-key, streamlined nature of the space.

❹ A kitchen can never have too much storage space for pots and pans. If you can, design the storage so that pots do not have to be stacked; shuffling through clattering pans is a nuisance over the long term. Here, runner-mounted shelves ensure easy access, even to items stored at the rear.

Most kitchen cabinets are 24 inches (61 cm) deep. In theory, that volume yields a good amount of storage space, but in practice only those items stored at the very front of the cabinet end up being used with any regularity, while those at the back are simply lost and forgotten. For this reason, many kitchen designers favor the use of drawers, which can be pulled open, making it easy to see and access everything inside. Another option is to install runner-mounted shelves that have a drawer-like action, although these must have a rim or rail to contain the movement of items when the shelf is pushed or pulled with too much force.

Wall space can be utilized for storage as long as the fittings don't encroach on headroom or intrude on the work area at counter height. Some manufacturers specialize in hanging rail systems that can be fitted out with accessories, such as paper towel dispensers, spice racks and holders for table napkins, as well as the hooks from which pots and pans can be hung. Even the simplest strategies, such as including cup hooks under a wall-hung cabinet or installing a slim shelf for the open storage of drinking glasses or spices, can make a notable difference to the efficiency of the kitchen, freeing up cabinet space and keeping frequently used items within easy reach.

❶ Shallow shelves are the most efficient storage system for grocery items, ensuring that almost every individual product is visible at a glance. Even quite a narrow space can be converted into a pantry.

❶

❷ Frosted glass doors give some hint of the depth behind their facade without exposing too much of the messy contents. These qualities can be useful in a small space where the solid surface of a wooden or laminated door could appear oppressive.

❷

❶

❷

❶ In a space-challenged kitchen, glass shelves mounted across a window provide extra storage space with only minimal disruption to the room's main source of natural light. A colorful bank of drawers serves two practical purposes — providing additional storage and supporting a long stainless steel countertop — but also makes a decorative contribution to the kitchen.

❷ A separate pantry is virtually a necessity in remote country houses where groceries must be stockpiled. Here, the pantry also incorporates a small amount of countertop space suitable for simple tasks, such as sorting through the shopping. A mobile island is stored here, but can be called into use in the nearby kitchen when cooking activity is at its most hectic.

❸

❹

❸ Appliance garages are a neat storage solution for small gadgets such as kettles and toasters. Fitted with power outlets and faced with either folding doors or a roller door as shown here, they allow instant and easy access. When in use, the appliances can take advantage of the surrounding work surfaces, but when the task is complete they can be simply pushed back into their storage niche, vacating the countertops.

❹ Open shelving provides cooking ingredients with a handy position close to the range. If these items were less readily accessible, they would probably end up lingering on the countertop between meals, taking up precious work space in a small kitchen.

4

DINING ROOMS

In the modern home, with its multipurpose rooms and open-plan living spaces, a table and some chairs are all it takes to construct an eating area. A dining room, though, is about more than mere function. If it is comfortable and inviting, and if it shows some heart and personality, it has the potential to revive a fast-disappearing yet inestimably valuable ritual: the family meal.

PERFECT DINING ROOMS

It may be more appropriate to talk about "dining areas" than "dining rooms." Unlike most other parts of the house, this is a space only rarely contained by four walls. In the contemporary home, meals are often shared among the merry disorder of a family living area, against the backdrop of a cheerfully busy kitchen or out in the open air of a verandah or courtyard.

Although it has become a part of the communal living space, the dining area deserves individual attention. A table wedged between a wall and a television cabinet will soon be forsaken in favor of a lap or a coffee table, and before long the family meal will have broken down into a series of individual sittings staggered throughout the day. By contrast, an area that has a reasonable amount of space around it, a distinct character and furnishings that are comfortable to use will draw people to the table and hold them together for as long as it takes to share a sociable mealtime — perhaps even longer.

PREVIOUS PAGES Many modern homes incorporate a variety of eating areas, including outdoor settings, casual family dining areas, kitchen breakfast bars and children's meal tables, sometimes all within the one open-plan space.

❶ In an open-plan area, a dining table needs a sense of place to feel like an inviting location for a meal. Here, a vibrant artwork and a richly colored rug define the space.

❶

❷ Natural materials appeal on an instinctual level. Here, oak shelving, an oak dining table and natural-fiber upholstery give the room texture and tonal warmth.

❸ In this dining room, antique furniture teams up with a contemporary painting by Stanley Palmer, ceramics by John Parker and a modern lacquer-finish bowl from Vietnam.

❹ This space incorporates three dining zones: a breakfast bar at the kitchen counter, a dining table for regular meals and an outdoor setting on the deck close to the barbecue.

❺ A change of floor height makes a gentle distinction between the kitchen and dining zones in an open-plan space.

SEPARATE ROOMS

A separate dining room is a rarity in the modern home. Where one does exist, it tends to be used for formal occasions and not for everyday meals. Because it is isolated from the day-to-day activity of the household, it can lack personality, so a deliberate effort should be made to imbue it with mood and character. The potency of color is an asset here: a coat of chocolate brown or a dashing scarlet feature wall will set the tone from the moment you pass through the door. And because you only spend limited amounts of time in this room, you can afford to be a little less practical and a little more fanciful with the decorating. This could be the place for a collection of boating or other memorabilia or a piece of tribal art that you're too timid to hang elsewhere.

It seems wasteful to maintain a room that is used only once or twice a month, and then only for a few hours at a time. Consider adapting your dining room so that it can do double duty, perhaps as a home office or a painting studio. A method of concealing these activities will have to be formulated. A screen could hide a computer and a printer; a dresser could be used to stow away art materials. Another option is to use the dining room as a library, lining the walls with bookshelves. It's a constructive use of an under-utilized space, but it also provides a warm and nostalgic backdrop for dining.

❶ This dining room has an unusual degree of flexibility. The opening at the far end connects the space with an adjacent living area, but wooden shutters fixed on the far side of the wall can be closed to give the room some separation. With the shutters open, the feeling is loose and casual; when they are closed, the space becomes more formal.

❶

❷ A room that is gentle acoustically is a naturally intimate space. Here, soft furnishings, such as floor-length curtains, plush carpeting and upholstered dining chairs, form a quiet and calm cocoon for formal entertaining. ❷

❶ This very contemporary dining room exhibits a high degree of decorating sophistication, with elements that appear and reappear in different manifestations contributing to a cohesive and distinctive personality for the space. The glass of the tabletop is picked up in the pendant light fitting. The black of the leather chairs reappears in the drawer fronts of the built-in cabinetry. The wood of the floor is used again as a sideboard countertop. A painting by Gary Waldrom incorporates both the colors and the qualities of those materials, including the water-like translucency of the glass and the density of the black surfaces.

❷ The doors can quite literally be closed on a separate dining room, which means a certain amount of decorating freedom can be indulged without fear of its overwhelming the rest of the house. This room, with its big, bright patterns and its pink and plum color scheme, would be hard to carry off in the more exposed environment of an open-plan area.

❸ This opulent setting could only exist in a separate dining room. Traditional Chinese furnishings look very much at home on a marble floor overlaid with a silk rug and against the backdrop of a silk tapestry.

❶

②

③

OPEN-PLAN ROOMS

Far more common than the separate dining room is an open-plan arrangement, either in the form of a purpose-designed living–dining or kitchen–dining space, or in the more ad hoc fashion of a family dining table tucked into a corner of the kitchen. The latter arrangement is almost always employed in houses where space is an issue, so your choices as to where to site the dining area are likely to be limited. Let common sense prevail. Try to avoid placing the table where it will obstruct movement around the kitchen and position it as far away as possible from a hot cooktop or oven. If the dimensions are truly cramped, a drop-down table attached to the wall and a set of folding or stackable chairs could be the only option.

❷

❸

❶ This open-plan space with its wall of glazing has a flowing feeling to it by day. At night, however, three discreet pendant lamps cast a cocoon of light around the table, creating an intimate ambiance for dining.

❷ Located in a broad section of hallway next to a staircase, this dining area could easily have been swallowed up by its surroundings. A large painting anchors the table and gives the space a distinct sense of purpose.

❸ The sofa in this living area turns its back on the dining table, setting a boundary between the two different zones.

Purpose-designed open-plan rooms work best when there is some form of demarcation between functions. A dining area ought to occupy a designated zone — it makes mealtimes more intimate and tends to make the clutter of a living room or the mayhem of the kitchen recede into the background, at least for as long as diners are gathered at the table. This distinction can be achieved by something as simple as a floor rug. If you're building from scratch, you could consider defining the dining area with a change in floor height or a different flooring material, perhaps a square of sisal set into a wooden floor.

A pool of light does the job even more effectively and with a greater sense of atmosphere. If you're installing downlights across an open-plan area, have them set up in such a way that different zones are controlled by different switches, so that the rest of the space can drop back into darkness once everyone is sitting at the table. Better yet, have lights fitted with dimmers so that they can be lowered once the meal gives way to glasses of wine and late-night conversation.

❶ In an open-plan living space, the dining table tends to have multiple uses. Certainly it's the place for family meals, but it can also be a sensible spot for children to work and play within sight of adults in the kitchen. The absence of walls also gives children extra room in which to run about and provides adults with plenty of space in which to gather during a social occasion.

❶

❷ In this refurbishment, a number of rooms were knocked together to form the desired open-plan living arrangement. Part of the wall was retained as a clever and unobtrusive way of marking the boundary between the kitchen and dining areas. The change to soft flooring in the dining zone helps with the demarcation, but also softens the acoustics. ❷

❶ The neutral palette and streamlined feeling are consistent throughout this open-plan space, but the hard surfaces of the kitchen give way to softer materials in the dining area.

❷ Given its seaside location and its owners' passion for minimalist interiors, there was no question that this penthouse would be designed with anything but wide-open living spaces. An L-shaped format keeps the mess of the kitchen far away from the dining area. It also ensures that while each of the functional zones occupies its own "space," they all benefit from the extraordinary ocean views.

❸ While it's important to create some definition between areas in an open-plan space, it is equally important to maintain aesthetic consistency. Without it, a combined living–dining or dining–kitchen area tends to feel messy and chaotic, no matter how well it is maintained. A counter with a raised servery clearly separates the kitchen and the dining area, but a thoughtful and comprehensive approach to furnishings — including wallpaper, drapery, upholstery and even tableware — gives the space a fresh feeling throughout.

❶

②

③

DINING OUTDOORS

Rooms that have a close relationship with the natural environment without being completely exposed to it are becoming increasingly popular in contemporary houses. Such rooms are inspired by traditional housing in parts of Asia, Africa and the Mediterranean. Walls of floor-to-ceiling windows achieve the effect, but glazed doors or wall panels that can be fully retracted go even further, merging the civilized comfort of the interior with the sensual delights of a neighboring garden space or an arresting view. Rooms such as these are an unadulterated pleasure in daylight hours but can be a little disconcerting at night, when those glazed expanses offer mirror reflections of the diners at the table. If the external space is lit — an urban nightscape, for example, or an artfully illuminated garden — the effect will be less noticeable. Otherwise, drapes or blinds are recommended.

❶ This formal dining area occupies a free-standing pavilion bordered on three sides by water gardens. The structure is influenced by traditional Balinese architecture. The pond provides a soothing vista, but also contributes on a quite practical level, keeping the room cool in the warmer months.

❶

❷ A wood-burning fireplace makes this an outdoor dining area that can be used in all seasons. The hard stone floor and solid concrete table build up a sense of substance and permanency, giving this outdoor room a very civilized, indoor character. That sense of civility is enhanced by the tailored approach to landscaping.

❷

❶

❶ In this dining area, panels of glazing are set between regularly spaced columns, a construction that summons up the feel of a garden colonnade or pergola even though the room is entirely enclosed.

❷ The soaring proportions of the space and the generous dimensions of the table setting are a match for the grandeur of the mountain landscape in which this house is set. In this region, the winters are bitterly cold and the summers stiflingly hot. A wall of glazing is protected by a deep external awning. In winter, when the sun travels low in the sky, its rays sneak under the awning and into the interior. In summer, when the sun is high overhead, the awning shades the glass, keeping the room cool.

❶

❶ This dining area is essentially an interior room but one with an unusual outdoor feeling. The high ceiling and the wall above the built-in bench are made from transparent perspex sheeting overlaid with wooden battens. Under the bench, the hardwood floor gives way to a border of loose pebbles. The result is a room with an oddly pleasing sense of impermanency.

❷ Furnished with its own bar, fireplace and barbecue, this dining area is classed by its owner as an "entertainment pavilion." Structurally, it is very much an interior space, but the use of glazing for walls and ceiling, the choice of a rugged stone floor and the very close proximity of the water feature reinforce the area's invigorating and refreshing outdoor character.

❷

FURNITURE

A table ought to be made from a material robust enough to cope with the odd drop of gravy or the sharp tine of a dropped fork. At the same time, it must have a tactile quality to it which ensures that those dining feel comfortable leaning forward to hear the conversation of someone sitting opposite. On top of all that, it must be a material that is easily cleaned. Wood is perfect for the purpose, unless of course it sports a finicky french polish, in which case it should be used only on special occasions or with the appropriate protective coverings. Stone and glass tend to be cold to the touch and are inclined to make a room uncomfortably noisy.

Chairs, too, must be conducive to long hours of fine food and good company, while being easy to maintain. Again, wood is the clear winner, especially when upholstered or supplemented with tie-on seat cushions. Wicker chairs make for easy sitting, too, though it can be difficult to clean the nooks and crannies of the intricate weave and they are notorious for wearing through under the pressure of frequent use.

❶ Upholstered seat cushions will prolong the life of these handsome wicker chairs.

❷ In a formal setting, upholstered chairs are elegant and comfortable. Be wary of using them at a family table unless they are fitted with loose covers that can be removed for cleaning.

❸ Antique chairs often receive more attention and have a greater impact in a contemporary space than in an authentic period room.

If upholstered chairs appeal, be sure to have them covered in a basic fabric and have them fitted with decorative slipcovers that can be removed for cleaning. The added advantage of slipcovers is that, when you tire of the original cloth or decide to change the look of the whole room, replacements in a new fabric are readily made.

Bench seating has a certain rustic charm, recalling both the ascetic appeal of the country farmhouse and the camaraderie of boarding-school dining halls. It offers the opportunity to spontaneously cater to larger groups, with diners cozying up together in an effort to fit more people around the table. It is perhaps more sensible, though, to limit the seating to two per bench so that either party can get up from the table without having to scramble over the knees of other diners. Benches have some practical advantages, too. For example, when not in use, the table could be pushed up against a wall, with the benches stashed beneath it to create a little extra living space in a small apartment or house.

❶ More commonly associated with outmoded suburban kitchens, the spatially compact eating nook is revisited here with surprisingly sophisticated results. A chic fabric has been used to upholster the built-in seating and the dining chairs.

❶

❷ These modern chairs have a traditional character suitable for a formal dining room. Upholstery studs are an unusual detail and will help to protect the edges of the seat back from wear and tear.

❸ They may be on permanent display, but the folding construction of these canvas chairs gives the room a pleasingly casual air.

❹ Popularly known as the "butterfly chair," Arne Jacobsen's distinctive and curvaceous plywood and tubular steel design was first made in 1955, yet still signifies something smooth and modern.

❺ A narrow table has the advantage of bringing guests close together.

perfect

BATHROOMS

Personality-charged bathrooms have taken the place of the bland, utilitarian spaces of old, which fulfilled a purpose but contributed nothing in terms of visual expressiveness. Tactile materials, sensual colors and interestingly unorthodox fittings create a distinctive identity, yet it's all for nothing unless sound planning first provides a room that functions efficiently and performs reliably.

PERFECT BATHROOMS

In most cases, bathroom design is an exercise in problem solving. The obligatory and often bulky items — bathtub, shower, basin and toilet — usually must fit into a room that is rather short on space. Factor in the location of windows and doors and the task of deciding which fixture goes where may become a very simple one: bathtub along the longer wall, toilet tucked away behind the door and so on.

If you're remodeling an old bathroom, you will also be limited by the existing positions of the plumbing. Pipes can, of course, be torn out and replaced in a different configuration, but this will add considerably to the cost of the work being done and could require approval from local authorities. Even in a brand-new bathroom, there will be some restrictions as to where you can locate the major fixtures. Installing water outlets on an external wall is easily done, but running the pipes through to internal walls can be an expensive matter.

These restrictions need not be oppressive. In fact, they can be liberating. Take the commonsense approach to the basic floor plan, then devote your creative energy to the more sensually rewarding decisions about color, surfaces and accessories.

PREVIOUS PAGES The floorplan of the bathroom is often dictated by structural necessities, but color and texture can be employed to put a personal stamp on the space, from the fresh and homely to the intensely exotic.

❶ The variety of bathroom fittings available has grown enormously in recent years. This tapered unit is a contemporary take on the classic pedestal basin. The surface-mounted faucets and attached towel rail make it a completely independent unit that, with the right plumbing, could be installed at some distance from the wall, a look that would suit a minimalist space.

❶

❷ Once it has been physically carved up into its component parts — shower stall, vanity unit, toilet — an already small bathroom can look positively cramped. Here, the space reads as a single, unbroken area, thanks to the use of clear glass shower walls and a distinctive wall treatment that extends right across into the shower stall.

❷

❶ This recessed area sets the scene for peaceful bathing. Wooden shutters are a sensible addition, ensuring a variable level of privacy.

❷ Recreating the look of a period bathroom is a relatively easy matter now that high-quality reproduction fittings are so readily available. Original pieces tend to be scarred with chips, scratches and stains, but companies specializing in resurfacing treatments can return them to their former glory with a fresh coat of enamel. Assuming the vintage fitting was picked up for next to nothing at a salvager's yard or a junk shop, the net cost of a resurfaced fitting is often lower than that of a brand-new reproduction fitting. It's up to you to decide whether the authenticity is worth the extra time and effort involved.

❸ Imposing a dividing wall some 6 feet (1.8 m) high on a space as small as a bathroom might seem a strange move, yet in this instance it was crucial to the room's success. The area in front of the wall, containing the vanity unit and the toilet, connects with the hallway. Behind the wall, a shower area links to the adjacent master bedroom. It's a clever way of creating a neat and restrained guest bathroom and a quite roomy master bath in the one space.

❶

②

③

❶

❶ Here, a fairly simple structure is given a strong personality with the use of contrasting materials and colors. A blue glass window panel, a blue glazed bowl for a basin and the use of white drawer fronts in the cabinetry pack a decorative punch.

❷ Sliding glass doors were used throughout this warehouse conversion as a way of creating intimate, domestic spaces without obliterating the industrial flavor of the building. Lower panels are frosted for privacy but upper panels are clear, allowing maximum light penetration and preserving the extended sightlines that confirm the space's massive dimensions.

❷

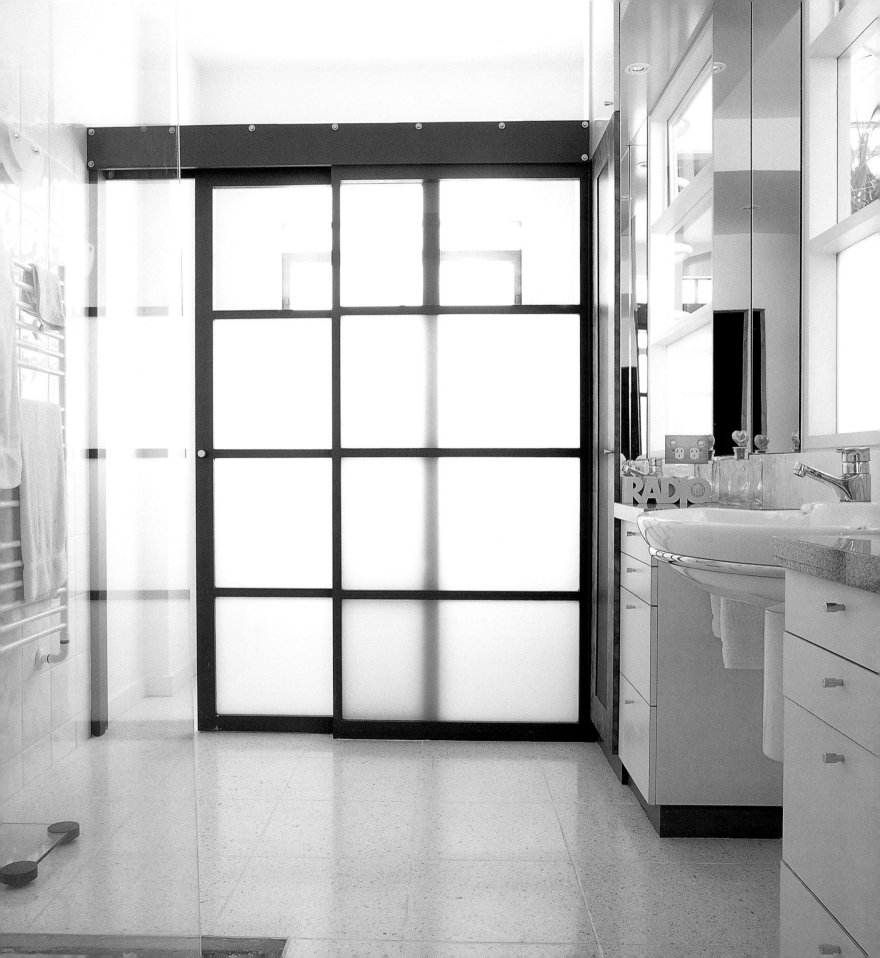

1

1 Here, twin vanity units are presented as two entirely self-sufficient work areas, each with its own mirror and storage space. Insets of studded flooring in front of each unit provide a nonslip surface.

2 A symmetrical layout tends to imbue a space with a sense of grandeur. It's also a commonsense approach to designing a bathroom that requires two work areas in the form of twin vanity units. Placing these units on opposite walls rather than alongside each other gives each user a zone of their own, so they are less likely to get under each other's feet.

2

SHOWERS

Showers come in three varieties: the old-fashioned over-the-bath arrangement, the conventional freestanding model and the rather more luxurious "wet room."

The selection of an over-the-bath shower is often motivated by necessity rather than preference. Obviously it's a space-saver, but if poorly handled it can also be an eyesore. The typically untidy version has a plastic or nylon shower curtain slung across it, which does only a fair job of containing splashes. If an over-the-bath shower is a must, consider having a glass screen fitted between the edge of the bath and the ceiling to form a more solid shower stall. It is a neater, cleaner, more attractive and more effective option than the tentlike rail-and-curtain arrangement.

❶

❷ Freestanding showers range from basic, prefabricated plastic shower trays with safety-glass surrounds to more elegant structures lined with beautiful tiles or offering secluded views.

❶ This master bathroom is a wet room: a waterproof space designed to get thoroughly soaked whenever the shower is used. The informality of this wet room is perfect for the bathroom's seaside location.

❷ Copper-clad walls and glass mosaic tiles completely outshine the modest proportions of this very humble over-the-bath shower.

❸ For the hedonist, this hi-tech shower has multiple showerheads, which can be used singly or in combination, as well as a computer program that will recall and activate your shower preferences.

❸

The fundamental requirement for any shower — no matter how opulent — is drainage. The floor must be laid so that water flows easily and quickly to the drainage outlet, without spilling out into the rest of the bathroom or, worse, into a carpeted bedroom or hallway. Be sure to question the tradespeople who are installing your shower about their experience in getting this crucial matter right. Errors can usually only be rectified by demolishing the existing floor and laying a new one, a costly, disruptive and time-consuming process.

Wet rooms are waterproof spaces fitted with one or more showerheads aimed to thoroughly drench the user. A wet room can take the form of a stand-alone room within a larger bathroom or it can function as a complete bathroom, incorporating wash basins and a toilet but with none of the fixtures or accessories that might be damaged by water. Wet rooms are conducive to shared showering experiences: a romantic option for couples and a playful way for a gaggle of children to scrub up together.

Color is one of the simplest, most effective and most cost-efficient ways to create a distinctive room identity. Here, blue tiles are used to clad the floor, the shower walls and the wall behind the toilet and bidet. The impact is bright and bold, and yet the use of colored rather than plain white tiles did not affect the overall budget. Cool blue is offset by accents of stainless steel in the fittings, toekick and vanity unit bulkhead.

There is a staggering array of shower fixtures available. The fixed overhead shower is less popular than it once was, partly because of its lack of flexibility and partly because it's guaranteed to wet your hair unless you wear a shower cap. It does, however, deliver a satisfying downpour of water. Showers on height-adjustable rails are valuable in a family situation, with each family member able to set the height of the showerhead to suit their size. Shower sets with flexible hoses that allow the showerhead to be used in a fixed position or as a hand-held unit also offer some versatility. When used in hand-held mode, the shower becomes a very useful place to wash children's hair, rinse sand-encrusted feet or even give the dog a spruce-up.

Water-saving showerheads are readily available. The very best offer a water consumption rate of about 2 gallons (7.5 liters) per minute, although a rate of up to 4 gallons (15 liters) per minute is still an improvement on most older models.

❶ Don't make the mistake of drawing up a floorplan that takes into account the dimensions of the fixtures, but fails to allow room to move among them. Leave at least 2 feet (60 cm) of clearance in front of the shower so that you can stand safely outside to test the water temperature before entering, as well as swing the shower door open with ease and finally step out and towel down without banging against walls and fixtures.

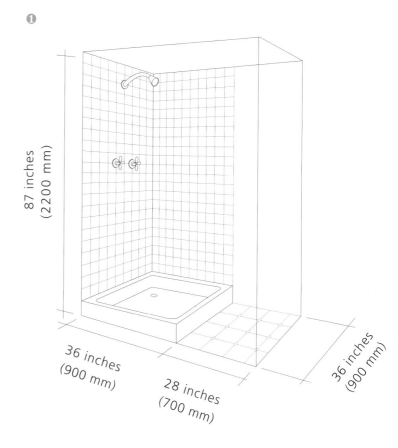

❶

87 inches (2200 mm)

36 inches (900 mm)

28 inches (700 mm)

36 inches (900 mm)

❷ Frameless glass shower screens are a fashion item in the modern bathroom. Their unadorned simplicity suits the predominating, clean-lined aesthetic. Lavender wall tiles are an interesting choice, softening the look of this bathroom.

❷

BATHTUBS

A bathtub offers more than mere functionality. For many, a soak in the tub is a chance to relax, unwind, and pamper oneself — perhaps even simply to enjoy some solitude.

Antique or reproduction claw-foot tubs, or the contemporary footed models they have inspired, have a graceful air. Being freestanding, they are also ideally suited to installation in the middle of the room or projecting at right angles from the wall. In a largish space, both of these options make a focal point of the bathtub.

Tubs designed to be fitted into solid surrounds are usually made of acrylic, steel or cast iron. Acrylic tubs are less expensive, lighter (and therefore more readily installed in upper-story bathrooms), but less effective at maintaining the heat of the bathwater. They won't chip as an enamel-coated metal tub can, but they may scratch or stain over time. The metal versions are more expensive and more heat-efficient, but prone to chipping over the long term. Their heavy weight may make them unsuitable for an upper-story bathroom.

Bathtubs can also be custom made, but this is highly specialized work which requires an experienced tradesperson. Usually, the structure is formed with concrete and then lined with tiles or, in some cases, wood.

❶ Patterned wallpaper and architectural detail make a suitable backdrop for a claw-foot tub. Those three components, together with drapes, a framed print and a rather refined reproduction chair, present this as a room for lingering in rather than a space in which to perform a few necessary ablutions.

❶

❷ The wide step and broad surrounds of this tub are far more massively proportioned than is structurally required. They do, however, make a feature of the gloriously deep bathtub and provide plenty of horizontal space for storage of accessories. They would also be excellent viewing ledges for adults supervising children at bathtime.

❷

❶

❶ The walls bracketing this spa bath feature mirror-image compositions of vanity units, cabinetry and storage niches. The intention was to showcase the tub, giving it and its tropical-courtyard vista a theatrical presence.

❷ Luxurious fittings and surfaces make a palace of this tiny apartment bathroom, but not without the assistance of a few decorating devices that give the illusion of extra space. Floor tiles laid on the diagonal trick the eye into believing there is just a little more width to the room than there really is, while the heated towel rail is set in a wall niche, ensuring the least possible intrusion upon the volume of the space. The mirror adds depth to the space and draws the eye away from the modest dimensions of the room. The lack of a pendant light fitting also increases the illusion of space.

❷

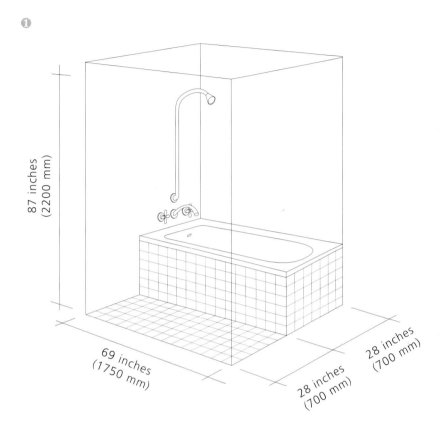

❶

87 inches
(2200 mm)

69 inches
(1750 mm)

28 inches
(700 mm)

28 inches
(700 mm)

❶ Bathtubs come in many shapes and sizes, but, whatever model you choose, you will need to allow extra room for getting into and out of the tub and perhaps even for dressing and undressing. A 2-foot (60-cm) deep strip of space, preferably along the long side, is the minimum.

❷ Like all the rooms in this beach house, the bathroom looks out to a blue horizon. Large tiles in a color to match the blue of the ocean were chosen because they required relatively less grouting than smaller tiles, reducing the internal distractions and keeping the focus on the view.

❶

❶ Reproduction period tubs such as this one offer some special luxuries. The tub's walls are considerably taller than those of a standard modern tub, allowing for a deliciously deep bath. The two cupped ends and the central placement of the drain also make it comfortable for two people to bathe at once.

❷ In an early 20th-century high-rise building, an original window and the vista it affords comprise the undisputed focal point of the bathroom. By positioning the tub directly below it, the designer has emphasized this point — and given the apartment owners a romantically cosmopolitan setting for bathing. Exposed plumbing and industrial wall lights highlight the bathroom's urban identity.

❷

VANITY UNITS AND BASINS

Hand basins can be wall hung, mounted on a pedestal or fitted into a piece of cabinetry. Within these categories, the choices range from the modest to the monumental.

Wall-hung basins are a sensible choice in a small bathroom. Some of these units are astonishingly tiny and can be installed almost anywhere, even in a corner. Visually, too, they have a space-saving impact. They do not take up floorspace and provide unobstructed sightlines through to the wall on which they are fixed, contributing to a sense of spaciousness.

Pedestal basins are almost as valuable in a small space, though this does not apply to the period models, which tend to have handsome shapes but bulky dimensions. Modern versions of the pedestal basin are extraordinarily diverse, from futuristic stainless steel bowls to organically shaped glazed ceramic styles.

❷

❸

❶ A bowl mounted on a plinth is a contemporary take on the classic pedestal basin, yet recalls the style of the old-fashioned wash basin and stand.

❷ A customized stepped plinth vanity in teak and marble and an antique mirror are suitably esoteric finishing touches in a resort-inspired guest bathroom.

❸ Wall-mounted taps reaching out from a wall-to-wall mirror, sleek basins, a glass slab countertop and handsomely striped teak cabinetry give a sophisticated and edgy look to a bathroom redesign in a Mies van der Rohe building.

Vanity units are produced in a variety of styles and are readily available wherever bathroom supplies are sold. Custom-made units can scale the heights of magnificence, stretching from floor to ceiling and wall to wall with twin basins, huge volumes of storage, in-built lighting and more. In short, your vanity unit can be as expensive and as extravagant as you choose.

Cantilevered or wall-hung vanities are increasingly popular, combining the storage capacity of a cabinet with the space-saving illusions of a simple wall-hung basin. Twin basins, championed by those who prefer not to wait in line while another family member applies their make-up or brushes their teeth, are being supplanted by a long trough-style basin. The long basin is overhung by two sets of faucets, but all water flows out through a single drain.

If you're adventurous and confident of your plumber's skills, consider using an unconventional object as a basin. With the right plumbing, a rustic old wash tub or a vintage water fountain can be converted into a strikingly original basin.

❶

❷

❶ A contemporary feel is created with a frosted glass basin, a glass counter and a highly reflective granite wall surface.

❷ The broad surrounds of these glass basins are used to keep everyday toiletries at the ready, eliminating the need for additional closed storage units.

❸ The mirrored wall on which this glass basin is mounted divides the shower stall from the toilet and shoots up dramatically into the cavity of a tall skylight. It also, of course, serves as a vanity mirror.

❸

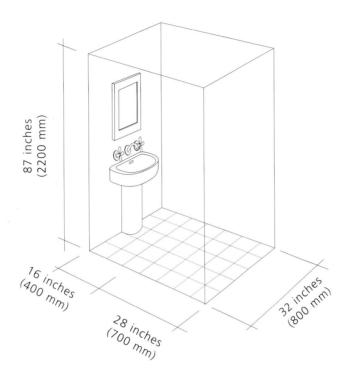

87 inches (2200 mm)

16 inches (400 mm)

28 inches (700 mm)

32 inches (800 mm)

❶

❶ Hand basins can be quite tiny objects, but, whatever their size, a certain amount of space in front and to either side of the unit must be included in the floorplan. The area where you stand while using the basin should measure at least 2 feet (60 cm) in depth. Elbow room is a more personal matter, but a total breadth of 2½ feet (75 cm) or more is preferable.

❷ This bathroom is presented very much as a furnished room and not at all as a utilitarian space. Accordingly, the vanity unit has been designed to look like a sideboard, complete with cane insets on the cupboard fronts. Wallpaper with a palm motif that is echoed in the embroidered towels, a cane-framed mirror and idiosyncratic light fittings lend a restrained tropical note to the room.

❷

LIGHTING AND VENTILATION

In most houses and apartments, the bathroom is a low-status room, occupying a corner of the building not overly endowed with natural light, ventilation or views. Views are a luxury, but light and ventilation are essential elements in the cramped, often steamy confines of a bathroom and must be introduced if they are not already in place.

Natural light coming in through a window is the most desirable light of all, not just because it makes a room look fresh and inviting throughout the day, but because it costs nothing and has absolutely no negative impact on the environment. If you're worried about privacy, consider replacing the clear glass with frosted or etched glass bought from a glazier, or applying a do-it-yourself frosting treatment that can be applied in situ. The obscured glass can be somewhat claustrophobic in a small room, but you have the option of applying frosting only to the portion of the

❶ Ceiling lights provide general illumination, but must be supplemented with additional task-oriented light fittings in a lowered ceiling above the vanity area.

❷ Twin skylights provide ample illumination and contribute a graphically decorative element in a warm but sleek space.

❸ A wash of daylight bestows a delightful freshness on this bathroom, a feeling enhanced by the clean lines of frameless mirrors, wall-mounted basins and a simple rectilinear oak storage unit.

window that presents a privacy problem: perhaps the lower set of panes in a multipaneled window or the bottom portion of a single piece of glass.

Artificial lighting should be considered in two categories: task lighting and ambient lighting. Task lighting comes into play around the vanity, where strong illumination is a necessity for shaving and make-up application. The very best set-up is to install light fixtures above the mirror and to either side, an arrangement that will result in a shadowless light.

The other functions of the bathroom can be carried out in less stark light. Downlights, wall-mounted uplights, or centrally located pendant lights — a must-have in authentic period bathroom refurbishments — will do the job well. Have them fitted with dimmers if you can, so that you have the option of a peaceful soak in the bathtub under soft lights.

Without adequate ventilation, the bathroom soon becomes an unpleasant and even unhealthy place. Ideally, a bathroom space would have good, big windows positioned to promote cross ventilation, which could be opened after every hot bath or steamy shower, but this is rarely the case and would be impractical in cooler climates. An adaptation of this idea is to install windows with multiple panels that can open separately. Hot air rises, so the top panels can be opened to let the steam out while the rest of the window remains closed, maintaining privacy and keeping the room free of direct breezes. Additional ventilation devices are more or less essential. In a house, a ceiling-mounted skylight that can be opened to aid the escape of hot, steamy air is an option that will also provide some extra natural light. Otherwise, electric exhaust fans mounted on the wall or ceiling with ducting leading to an external vent are a practical alternative.

❶ Solid shower walls block out light, usually making it necessary to illuminate the shower stall with artificial lighting at any time of day. Here, walls made from glass bricks allow available daylight to penetrate the interior of the shower. The glass-brick construction also makes possible the unusual circular shape of the shower, a form that could not easily have been produced in conventional glass.

❶

❷ Set back into a niche alongside the bathroom's only window, this vanity will always require supplementary lighting. The need for artificial task lighting is met by ceiling-mounted downlights. It's a neat approach to lighting in a serene and subtly furnished bathroom.   ❷

❶

❶ A good supply of natural light makes a bathroom feel clean and fresh, yet the clear glass windows which make that possible are at odds with the requirement for privacy. Textured glass bricks are one way of solving the problem. They obscure the view of the interior from the outside while facilitating the penetration of daylight.

❷ This well-equipped vanity unit could be described as a bathroom work-station. A long run of cabinetry has a large storage capacity and supports twin basins for maximum efficiency. Twin mirrors are augmented by two magnifying mirrors on extendable arms. Ceiling-mounted downlights provide task lighting, while wall sconces contribute a more gentle, ambient light.

❷

STORAGE

The items that need to be stored in a bathroom tend to be small: medicines, cosmetics, bottles of perfume, grooming tools and so on. Almost always, these can be contained in shelves or cabinets of a very shallow depth. In fact, items stored on broader shelves or in deeper cabinets are likely to be lost and forgotten.

Look to the walls above the bath and the toilet for extra storage space. Often, these can be fitted with narrow shelves or a slim cabinet, but don't install anything too wide or you risk knocking your head with irritating regularity. The wall cavities themselves can be a storage opportunity for those undertaking new building work. Shelves or a cabinet can be installed so that they occupy a niche in the wall without jutting out into the body of the bathroom.

❷

❸

❶ Teaming raw materials in sophisticated forms is a warm and organic version of a minimalist aesthetic. Here, concrete counter-tops combine with finely burred bleached bird's-eye maple cabinetry and a wall washed with terra cotta.

❷ Be vigilant in looking for unusual storage opportunities. Empty wall cavities can be used to provide storage niches such as this one.

❸ Freestanding storage is not a common sight in the bathroom, but, if space allows and if the piece is waterproof, it can be both a functional and a decorative asset.

❶

❶ This handsome mahogany cabinetry is one half of an island unit that comprises back-to-back vanity units. On this, the "his" side, the emphasis is on storage capacity. Drawers on both sides of the unit are fitted with electrical sockets so that the appliances they contain are ready to use.

❷ A bank of cabinetry functions as both storage space and partition screen in a surprising and stimulating refit of a Victorian-era room. The nooks and niches of the unit provide places to stow essential toiletries, platforms for the display of art and windows that allow glimpses through to the far wall. The reverse side of the unit functions as a headboard for the bath. On the left, a mirrored panel is a sliding door that opens on to a walk-in closet.

❷

6

perfect

BEDROOMS

More than simply a place to sleep, the bedroom is a place in which to get away from the household clamor and enjoy precious moments of solitude. It must, therefore, offer not just privacy, but also intimacy and comfort. Furnish the space with ample storage, good lighting and a sturdy bed, then let your personal taste dictate the rest.

PERFECT BEDROOMS

Ideally, a retreat to the bedroom should involve a physical move away from the busiest areas of the house. You should be able quite literally to leave the hustle and bustle of the kitchen or the family room behind you, withdrawing to a relatively quiet space located in a far corner or on a second story.

Where such an ideal is not practicable, however, a few simple devices can help to create a more peaceful space. Double-glazed windows and old-fashioned wooden shutters will cut down on external noise. Acoustic insulation installed in wall cavities can be used to muffle sounds from adjacent rooms. If the location or use of the room undermines the sense of seclusion — for example, if it's at the front of the house on a busy street, or if it's a bedroom occupied by two or more children — consider hanging a canopy over the bed, letting the "walls" of fabric form an even more intimate mini-zone within the bedroom itself. Four-poster beds are designed to hold a canopy, but modern beds can be treated in a similar way simply by hanging lengths of fabric from ceiling-mounted hooks or rods.

Waking in a room filled with the softer light of morning is a gentle and calming way to start the day, so it's preferable to locate a bedroom on the eastern face of the building. Bedrooms that face west will soak up a lot of late afternoon sun, which can make them uncomfortably hot on summer nights.

PREVIOUS PAGES Small bedrooms benefit from simple furnishings and a lack of embellishment, but that pared-down approach can give a characterless result. In this bedroom, a vintage tone of green on walls and ceiling brings the room to life.

❶ All members of the family need to be able to shut themselves away from the others every now and then, but in hot weather, closing the bedroom door can create an uncomfortably stuffy atmosphere. By angling the blades on the internal louvered door, the users of this bedroom can maintain their privacy without inhibiting the flow of air around the house.

❶

❷ A subdued color scheme and a limited palette of materials keep distractions to a minimum, imbuing this small bedroom with a sense of orderliness and calm. A sliding door of opaque glass means that the bed can be screened off from the neighboring dining area without completely obstructing the flow of light from the bedroom's broad windows.

❷

❶

❷

❶ This eclectic selection of furniture and belongings holds together because of the repetition of touches of gilt and delicate, faintly Oriental angles and curves through-out the various pieces.

❷ Custom-made cabinetry meets the storage needs of the bedroom without undermining the elegant character of the space.

❸ Layers of soft furnishings create a soft and sumptuous environment. Ensure coherence by letting a single pattern dominate. An over-abundance of prints distracts the eye and can make the space look unkempt.

❸

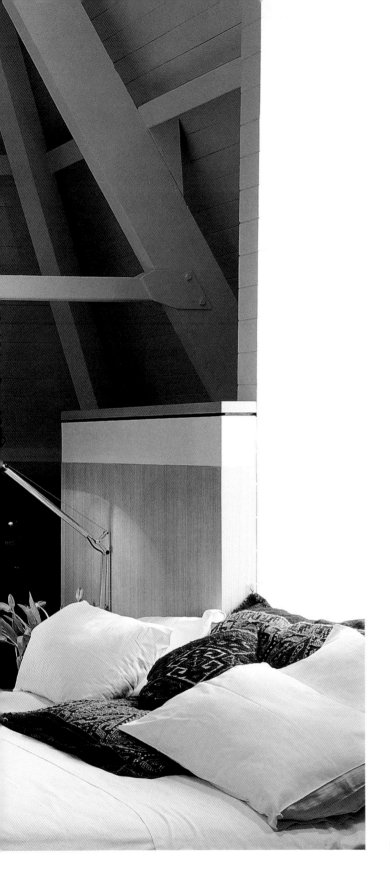

❶

❶ The height and orientation of attic bedrooms usually guarantee a certain level of privacy, making it possible to install extra-large windows like those in this room. Make sure that ceiling-mounted lighting is installed at the time the room is being built, because a lack of roof space will make later electrical additions almost impossible.

❷ This unusually shaped room offers desirable seclusion, but its awkward dimensions require creative solutions. The uniform built-in cabinetry of the study area and the bedside storage consolidate the room, enabling the owners to utilize this potentially useless space.

❷

1 The desire for large expanses of glazing often clashes with the need for privacy in a built-up environment. A window treatment that comprises one light translucent fabric and one heavy block-out fabric works well in such situations. By day, the sheer fabric lets in most of the light while obscuring views of the interior from outside the building. At night, the heavier fabric can be drawn across for complete seclusion.

1

2

2 The relatively small size of bedrooms in most 19th-century buildings leaves little room to install an adjoining bathroom. The owners of this house solved that problem by turning an adjacent bedroom into a lavishly proportioned master bath, complete with working marble fireplace.

3 This master bedroom has an unusually strong sense of rarefied isolation. It is physically set apart from the main body of the house, accessible only via a bridge lined in poly-carbonate sheeting and glass louvers. The light and airy quality of the space, established in the bridge and reinforced by extensive use of louvered windows in the bedroom itself, makes it possible to use the deep tones of terra cotta and blue that would have swamped a smaller, darker room.

3

❶ A bedroom is supposed to be a very intimate, very personal space — one that permits a level of decorating freedom that may not be feasible in more public areas of the house. This particular flight of fancy incorporates a water feature and a meditative interior garden. The symmetry of the fittings contributes a temple-like character to the space.

❷ The eyrie retreat of a bedroom balcony is a world away from the hustle of the house and offers the opportunity for restorative isolation. The sense of spaciousness in this bedroom is increased by the inclusion of an unglazed internal window that looks down over the ground-floor dining area. The open structure makes the most of the available light, but poses problems for acoustic privacy.

❸ An addition to a 1950s vintage seaside house, this new guest suite was built with lightweight materials. The loose, informal structure conjures the liberatingly simple structures of childhood holiday houses. However, because beds can look and feel odd unless set against something solid, a wall has been installed, becoming the grounding element that gives the space visual stability.

❶

❷

❸

❶ Bedrooms filled with heirloom furniture and treasured possessions are a source of great comfort to some. Avoid an amateurish quality by maintaining some order within the scheme. Here, matched pairs of bedside tables and lamps and a collection of similarly framed pictures are the stable elements around which the more whimsical pieces can be arranged.

❷ Achieving a strong sense of personality in a bedroom without intruding on its tranquillity is a matter of delicate balance. While soft neutrals and blushing pinks set a calm mood in this bedroom, its playful twist on symmetry — matching paintings in different colors and a pair of blinds, one pink, the other white — reveals a quietly quirky identity.

❸ Bedrooms in modern spec-built houses tend to be fairly characterless spaces, lacking architectural detail. A careful arrangement of personal items, such as this collection of antique furniture pieces and artworks, can avoid potential blandness.

LIGHTING

Bedroom lighting is a delicate matter. Strong illumination is vital for certain activities, such as reading in bed or dressing, but can be harsh and unrestful when the bedroom is being used as a place to relax and unwind. Don't rely on a standard central ceiling light to satisfy the functional requirements of a bedroom lighting scheme. Because of its location, the central light fitting will actually produce shadows where good light is needed. Inevitably, you will be standing between the light source and the wardrobe, casting the dressing area into shade. Nor will the light shine directly on the pages of your book or newspaper, falling instead on the back of it.

A good solution is to use multiple downlights, installed so that different banks of light fittings are assigned to different switches. That way you can have strong illumination over the wardrobe area where one partner is getting dressed, while the other partner rests in bed, untroubled by bright lights.

If you're not installing a whole new lighting scheme, then replace the globe in your central ceiling light with a low-wattage bulb or have a dimmer fitted and use the overhead light for ambient purposes only while looking to other solutions for task lighting. An inexpensive and effective idea is to have your closet fitted with the kind of door-activated striplights often employed in kitchen pantries. If your budget allows, consider having those striplights fitted both high, where they will cast light onto your racks of clothes, and at floor level, where shoes are often stored.

❶ A run of casement windows set high into the wall above the bed lets in the light without compromising privacy.

❷ Floor-to-ceiling glazing makes the most of all the available daylight.

❸ Mounting reading lamps on the wall above the bed keeps clutter off the bedside cabinets, but does limit your options for rearranging the floorplan later on.

❹ Despite their rigid construction, wooden shutters offer greater flexibility than fabric drapes when it comes to light control. By changing the angle of the blades, this naturally light room can be shaded from the first rays of morning or protected from the intense, hot afternoon sun.

When using lamps in bedrooms, it's a common mistake to confuse the decorative with the functional. Lamps designed to emit an ambient aura of light — including the very traditional pedestal base lamps with fabric shades — are unsuitable for reading and may damage your eyesight if used long term. Purpose-designed reading lamps must be flexible and cast good directional light on whatever you are looking at, be it a novel, a diary or some needlework. Some come fitted with switches that allow the light to be set at varying levels of brightness, an excellent option in the bedroom because it means they can be used for mood-setting as well as functional purposes.

This bedroom has been designed to create an aura of after-dark glamour. Carefully selected luminous materials — mirrored insets on either side of the bed, silk taffeta drapes and bed cover, and silver leaf on the dressing table — all pick up the sparkle of lamplight and contribute to the starlit mood.

❶

❶ An elevated ceiling faced with glazing admits as much natural light as possible. Wall-mounted sconces produce a diffuse glow that serves as ambient light.

❷ Louvered windows usually fulfill two purposes, letting in light and facilitating air flow. Here, fitted with yellow rather than the standard clear glass blades, they serve a third, decorative role.

❸ In a small space, recessed ceiling downlights and wall-mounted reading lamps positioned high above the bed provide a streamlined solution to functional and mood lighting.

❸

STORAGE

As luxurious as it may seem, a very personalized approach to clothes storage usually results in the most space-efficient solution. If you're having built-in closets made — or if you're trying to make the most of an existing built-in — take stock of your clothes and look at the proportion of shirts, jackets, pants and skirts you need to store in relation to the number of full-length garments such as coats and dresses. Shorter items usually only require a drop of about 3 feet (1 m) compared to the roughly 6-foot (1.8-m) drop needed for longer garments, meaning you can hang one rack of clothes above another, thus doubling your storage area in the same amount of floorspace.

❶ Investing in customized joinery is money well spent in a cramped bedroom, especially if the unit is to fill an awkward gap. It ensures that every bit of space is utilized, and that every item in the closet is neatly housed.

❷ In a large bedroom, a partition screen serves both as a headboard for the bed and, on the reverse side, an open closet space. The avenue between the screen and the rear wall functions as a modest dressing room.

❸ An unusual piece of cabinetry has multiple functions: a dividing wall and a handsome, graphic backdrop for the bedroom, it also provides generous storage niches.

The advantage of built-in closets over freestanding wardrobes is that they can present a seamless facade. Although they may cover as much floorspace as a comparable assortment of free-standing furniture, they don't present the same kind of visual obstruction. As a result, the room tends to feel more spacious and easier to navigate. Built-in closets do, however, limit your options for the placement of other pieces of furniture, so take time in deciding exactly where they should be installed.

❶

❷

❶ It seems a shame to disturb the elegance of a well-furnished bedroom with a television set, yet watching favorite movies in bed is a modern-day indulgence. Scout around for an appropriate piece of furniture, such as this antique cabinet, that can house audiovisual equipment while also harmonizing with the style of the room.

❷ Maximize storage capacity by taking built-in units all the way to the ceiling.

❸ The area above a freestanding wardrobe can be a wasted space, but here it has been used to show off a collection of basketware.

❸

Whether you opt for built-in or freestanding clothes storage, focus on making frequently used items as accessible as possible. If you often find yourself wasting time by shuffling through a disorganized collection of shoes, handbags or T-shirts, then find a way of prioritizing these in your storage scheme, even if the solution seems unconventional. The shoes, for example, might be stored on sliding shelves at waist height in the closet rather than being stowed at floor level. The handbags could be hung singly on a series of hooks mounted on a door or even on a wall. The T-shirts, rather than being crammed into an over-stuffed drawer, might be tucked into pigeon holes, one T-shirt per niche.

The unobtrusiveness of a built-in closet is its greatest asset. In this instance, wall-to-wall, floor-to-ceiling cabinetry furnishes the bedroom with enormous storage capacity, without overwhelming the space or inhibiting its exotic styling. The simple molding on the doorfronts is the decorative detail needed to unite the cabinetry with the bedroom's other, more opulent furnishings.

❶

❶ A headboard with built-in storage ledges recalls the style of North African architecture. The lower shelf keeps books and trinkets close to hand, while the less-accessible upper shelf is used for long-term storage, with items being stored in suitcases that may otherwise lie empty for months or even years. These can contain blankets, woollens, special-occasion garments and other items that only need retrieving once or twice a year. If the suitcases are particularly handsome or particularly old, they can be treated as a decorative feature in their own right.

❷ Recessed shelving offers room for storage without impinging on the floor area, an important consideration in a space-starved bedroom.

❷

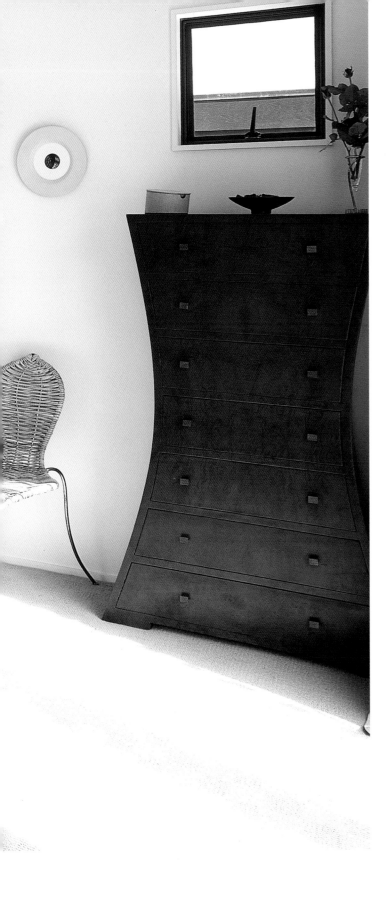

THE BED

CHOOSING A MATTRESS

The mattress on which you sleep has an enormous impact on your physical and mental well-being. When a mattress fails to support the weight of your body, your muscles are forced to compensate, leaving you stiff and sore in the morning. Worse still, a restless night of tossing and turning can mean you miss out on the deep sleep that nourishes and rejuvenates mind and body.

When setting out to buy a mattress, start by separating the concepts of "support" and "comfort." The former is a standard that all mattresses should meet. The latter is entirely a matter of personal preference.

Mattresses can be as simple as a chunk of latex rubber or as specialized as a natural bedding mattress made from blends of wool, cotton and coconut fibers, but the great majority have a sprung construction. The old-fashioned hourglass-shaped springs used over a century ago are still the standard in budget-priced mattresses. Better-quality mattresses use a variety of more complex modes of construction, each with its own advantages to suit different sleeping arrangements and body weights. The basic rule, though, is that the smaller and more numerous the coils, the better the mattress will be able to support you.

Finding a bed to match the eccentricity of the other furnishings in this bedroom would have been quite a challenge. Instead, the owners opted for the simplicity and flexibility of an ensemble mattress. An upholstered base smooths the look and saves the bed from the anonymity common to much mass-produced furniture.

The "comfort" in a mattress is provided by the padding around the springs. Again, the options are many and varied, from simple and inexpensive synthetic fillers to the luxury of latex, which is made from the sap of rubber trees and has natural antibacterial and antifungal properties. As long as you are sure that you are getting good support from your mattress, the choice of comfort level is completely up to you.

You really need to spend at least 15 minutes on a mattress to get a true impression of the support and comfort it offers. Take a book or magazine with you when you go mattress shopping as an incentive for laying there a bit longer.

Having bought the best mattress you can afford, you must then take good care of it. Even out the wear by turning it over from side to side and end to end every few weeks. At least once a year, take it off the bed and leave it out in the sun to air. Mattresses should be replaced every six to ten years.

❷

❸

❶ The unusual design of this piece expresses the modern bed's dual role as recreational center and sleeping venue. The broad surrounding platform also serves as a spot to perch comfortably.

❷ Antique beds dressed in period linen can look like museum pieces. Unless authenticity is your goal, it's preferable to modernize the look with plain white bed linen.

❸ Using twin mattresses to form a shared bed makes it possible to combine different comfort levels, satisfying both parties.

DRESSING THE BED

Antique beds are at their best when dressed in a style to suit the period in which they were made. If you're besotted with a certain bed, but worried that it will end up looking like a museum piece, the best approach is to use the appropriate quilts or canopies, but all in cool, clean white. The all-white scheme will camouflage the extra flounces and give the bed a fresher, more contemporary look.

Throughout the 1970s and 1980s, the duvet was probably the most popular style of bed cover, and with good reason: it is lightweight yet warm and makes bed-making a simple task. Recently, though, there has been a return to vintage fashions in bedclothes. Layers of quilts, coverlets and bedskirts — a look that can be either pretty and feminine or grand and formal — are best suited to modern beds that have a nostalgic feel, be they straightforward reproductions or simply designs that echo the shapes and materials of traditional beds. The smartly tailored look of sheets folded over blankets is a good match for clean-lined contemporary bed designs.

❶ The scallop-edged Marcella quilt is an authentic match for the antique French furnishings in this bedroom.

❷ Bolster cushions enhance the traditional European styling of an Italian-made sleigh bed, while throwing a dash of color into this very classic bedroom setting.

❸ Indulge in the purchase of extra pillow-cases in colors and prints that complement the main set of bed linen. It's a comparatively inexpensive way of creating a generous yet tailored look for the bed.

❶

❶ Including an armchair in the bedroom provides the occupant with a place to enjoy a quiet cup of coffee first thing in the morning, or sit down to go through the mail, or curl up with a book on a lazy afternoon. In this way, the bedroom functions as a private sitting area in a busy, noisy household.

❷ With the addition of a sheer fabric canopy hung from a simple curtain rod, an ordinary ensemble bed can be transformed into a romantic setting.

❶

❶ There's nothing spare, streamlined or monochrome about the country look. Collect little home-made cushions embellished with applique, embroidery, fringing and patchwork and toss them onto the bed to create a joyful cacophony of color, texture and pattern.

❷ A brass bed, a multitude of vibrant prints and a generous scattering of hand-stitched quilts conjure the colorful and exuberant style of the iconic country house, immediately bestowing a warm and friendly mood on any bedroom.

❷

7

HOME OFFICES

Whether it's a room apart or just a corner of the kitchen, the space devoted to work or study should have at least some of the discipline of a professional office. Avoid mass-produced modular furniture if it doesn't suit your decor, but stick to the basic principles of good lighting, efficient storage and reliable technology.

PERFECT HOME OFFICES

Almost every home has an office space of some kind. There will always be tax to do, accounts to oversee, bills to pay — routine paperwork that is best done in well-ordered surrounds with documents filed neatly and stored securely. There may also be short stretches of time when a family member has to bring work home from the office, maybe for a couple of weekends in a row during a busy patch, or perhaps for as long as a year as a new mother makes the transition back from maternity leave by working part of the week at home.

Increasingly, though, the spare bedroom is becoming the launching site of small businesses and fledgling consultancy services. In these cases, the design of the home office ought to match the level of confidence and commitment with which the new venture is being pursued. This is not to say that a home office should have the look and feel of the corporate environment found in a high-rise office tower. It's a simple matter of giving the space the respect it deserves, rather than allowing it to become a ramshackle repository of mismatched furniture discarded from other rooms in the house. Minimalist or feminine, monastic or bright and buzzy, your office should offer you efficiency, comfort and pleasure.

PREVIOUS PAGES Whether the style is somber and traditional or dynamic and urban, the fundamentals for home offices remain the same: ample lighting, abundant storage, sufficient work surfaces and a chair that offers comfort and support.

❶ This handsomely appointed office looks nothing like a modern workstation, yet is perfectly well equipped for its task. Walls lined with bookcases do a marvelous job of insulating the room against distracting noise generated elsewhere in the house.

❶

LOCATION

A room apart, away from noise and distraction, is the ideal for most people working from home. It may mean the sacrifice of a spare bedroom or a dining room, or it may compel the transformation of an attic, garage or shed. Your budget may not allow for the luxury of a full refurbishment, but for you to work happily and healthily, the space must at least be well lit, well ventilated, well supplied with electricity and telephone connections, comfortably warm in winter and cool in summer and capable of being appropriately secured.

If a separate room is not available, it will be necessary to consider a space-sharing arrangement. A workstation can be installed in a variety of different rooms in the house, each with its own advantages and disadvantages.

In some respects, the bedroom is the perfect spot for a workstation, given that it is comparatively under-utilized during the day. It can, however, make for a depressing scenario, as it invades your personal sanctuary, making it difficult to switch off from work and even disrupting the sleep patterns of those already prone to bouts of insomnia. Installing the office set-up within a custom-made cabinet, built-in or freestanding, would give you the option of shutting all the work away behind closed doors when it's time to relax. A decorative screen could likewise camouflage the workstation when not in use.

The dining room presents an inviting opportunity, equipped as it is with a table that can do service as an expansive work surface. This option may work for singles or couples happy to eat dinner on their laps when there's work in progress, but workers with families will need to clear the table at the end of each day, an interruption to work flow that could prove an irritation in the long run.

❶ Staircases perform an important structural function, but can be the cause of wasted space on the lower level. A century ago, that nook under the stairs was commonly used as a linen closet or a small coatroom. Today, it proves a neat location for a well-organized office area.

❶

❷ Most people prefer at least some acoustic privacy, if not complete seclusion, when they are at work. If you have the luxury of dictating your own floorplan as part of a refurbishment or a new building project, try to locate a home office at some distance from the main living areas. ❷

Living rooms and kitchens could also provide space for a workstation. However, the proximity to household activity that would make such a location desirable for anyone doubling up on professional and family duties could also be a drawback when there is a need for concentration.

Slightly more out-of-the-way places — little nooks that are often wasted — can prove more serviceable than any of the space-sharing arrangements suggested above. An alcove, a broad landing or the pocket of space under a staircase is perfect for a compact home office. Given that these locations are always small and often awkwardly shaped, you'd be well advised to consider a built-in workstation that can be customized to make best use of the available space.

The other alternative is to free yourself of any permanent set-up and opt instead for a remote office. A cordless phone and a notebook computer mean that the living room sofa, the porch steps — even the bed, if you're so inclined — can be your office for an hour or two.

❶ Easy to see at a glance and always accessible, open storage is a sensible choice for the jumble of files, reference material, stationery, orders, bills and tax records that are an inevitable feature of the home office.

❷ Built-in cabinetry is an extremely reliable way of fitting comfortable work spaces and maximum storage capacity into a limited volume of space. This set-up was incorporated into a kitchen refurbishment.

❸ Designed with an eye to space-saving strategies, this built-in office has an L-shaped worktop along two walls. A large mirror helps to counteract feelings of confinement.

FURNISHING

Years spent working in the impersonal surrounds of a big city office block can lull you into a decorating stupor from which it is surprisingly hard to wake. It's very easy to fall back on the gray metal filing cabinet/laminate desk top/plastic pen holder approach to workstation decorating, despite the fact that you now have the freedom to store your papers in wicker trays, set up your computer on an old military campaign table and stash your pens in a Georgian tea caddy.

Of course, you might feel that a conventional, purpose-built desk setting helps you to feel professional. It's a valid stance, especially if you expect to see clients in your home office who might otherwise be visiting other suppliers or service providers in more orthodox office spaces.

❶

❷ If, however, this is not an issue, you should furnish your office as you would any other room in your house — in a style that makes you feel confident, comfortable, secure and stimulated. Almost any piece of furniture can be used in a home office, provided that it satisfies or can be adapted to meet ergonomic requirements. So, if your house is filled with grand antiques, opt for something like a leather-topped writing desk. If it has a country-house feel, consider an old farmhouse dining table. For a modern home, choose something sleek and chic.

❸

❶ This handsomely appointed space proves that purpose-built office furniture can be designed to suit a domestic interior. The customized units ensure that the ergonomic requirements are met and that storage is both abundant and accessible.

❷ Floor-to-ceiling bookshelves have a scholastic charm. They also have another, perhaps unexpected, advantage in that they provide very effective acoustic insulation.

❸ Where space is tight, a home office must be flexible. This streamlined room is amply furnished with work surfaces and storage yet could easily swap roles to become a smart spare bedroom.

EQUIPMENT

The average home computer set-up requires several power sockets. Two would be the bare minimum — one for the hard drive and one for a printer — but you'll also probably need to power speakers or an external modem, a scanner, a fax and an answering machine. A lumpy conglomerate of double adapters plugged into a single outlet is not a suitable way to handle the problem. Either use a multisocket power board or have an electrician install multiple outlets at the wall.

At present, most home office set-ups use a minimum of two telephone lines: one for the phone and one dedicated to internet connection. Depending on your patterns of usage, you may want to run your fax on the phone line or on the line used to connect to the internet — or invest in a third line to ensure you're working at maximum capacity at all times.

Multiple telephone lines may soon be a thing of the past. Standard phone lines can only carry a certain amount of traffic at any one time. This means that if you're using a line for internet connection, you will not be able to make or receive phone calls on that same line. Broadband technology offers increased traffic flow. In the UK and the USA, Asymmetric Digital Subscriber Lines (ADSL) are emerging as a popular form of broadband. ADSL can be used to transmit both voice signals and digital signals. In other words, you could be talking to a client at the same time as you receive e-mails or download information. This capacity means that you don't need to dial up your internet service provider to connect to the internet — the connection is effectively "on" at all times.

❶ Even something as simple as a feature wall painted in a favorite hue can be the inspirational element that every good home office needs. Color also enhances the personality of a room that is often furnished in a sparse, inexpensive and utilitarian way.

❶

❷ Classically styled architectural features and a range of comfortable furnishings make this a space that can function as either serious office or elegant reading room. Thick carpeting and a majestic bookcase also help to soundproof this office, further enhancing its role as a serene sanctuary.

❷

ERGONOMICS

Whether your home office is a corner of the kitchen or a purpose-built pod, you must adhere to the recommended ergonomic guidelines or risk constant trouble with headaches, back pain and eyestrain.

THE KEYBOARD

When using the keyboard, your forearms should be more or less parallel to the floor, wrists in a neutral position, fingers dropping lightly on the keys.

THE MONITOR

Position the monitor at arm's length with the screen tilted slightly upward. The top half of the monitor should be positioned at eye level so that you don't drop your head or hunch your shoulders while working. Avoid glare by positioning the screen at right angles to the window. Don't be tempted to face the window so that there is bright light directly behind the monitor; the variation in light levels between the screen and the outside world can cause troublesome eyestrain.

THE CHAIR

While you can be creative about your choice of desk, a purpose-designed work chair with adjustable seat height, arm-rests and backrest is a must. However, even an ergonomically designed chair can be as bad for your back as an upturned bucket unless it is adjusted to suit your personal requirements. The backrest should support your lower back snugly and be reclined just slightly to discourage you from leaning over the desk. The seat height should be adjusted so that your thighs are more or less parallel to the floor with your feet resting flat on the floor or on a footrest.

❶ A desk lamp is essential, even in a room that has a good natural light source. Anyone using the desk is likely to cast a shadow over their work if they are relying on ceiling-mounted lights alone. A light source sited on the table can be positioned so that light falls directly onto the page.

❶

❷ Even the most unorthodox of tables can be used as a desk provided it is accompanied by an adjustable chair that can be raised or lowered to suit the height of the work surface.

❷

8

OUTDOOR SPACES

Houses and their gardens work best when the boundaries between them are blurred. Let living spaces drift out into those shaded, fragrant corners and let the soft visions and fresh breezes of the garden flow back into the house. In doing so you will bring life to your interiors and sophistication to those green spaces.

PERFECT OUTDOOR SPACES

There's much to be gained by drawing the outdoors into the interior of the house and letting the house itself spill out into the surrounding environment. In practical terms, it increases living space without the costs and hassles of a fully fledged extension. Even a picnic rug and a couple of cushions tossed out on the lawn can effectively provide another space in which to relax, an alternative that might be rewardingly liberating in situations where privacy and solitude can be hard to come by, say for the residents of a tiny worker's cottage. And by increasing the options, a livable outdoor area gives a house some breathing space. Suddenly those walls aren't so confining, or that ceiling so oppressive. There's a sense of optimism and freedom that comes from sitting in a room with a wall-to-wall length of folding doors pushed back to let in the sights, the sounds and the smells of a garden, and a sense of joyful independence associated with a meal prepared, cooked and enjoyed in the outdoors at a civilized table setting.

PREVIOUS PAGES Paved areas have the solid foundations of a livable space. They function on a practical level, providing a firm footing for furniture pieces, but they also give the area a dressed look that puts it on a par with interior rooms.

❶ Pebbles are an excellent ground cover in areas where lawn is not an option, for example in the shaded interior of a walled courtyard. Paving stones provide a more stable walkway than the pebbles and draw the eye to the space's feature piece.

❶

❷ ❸
❹ ❺

❷ Comfortable furnishings can turn a verandah or porch into an extension of the house's living spaces.

❸ Paving that provides a sturdy surface for an outdoor table setting and a pergola that ensures good shade give this area the status of an outdoor room.

❹ In this lavish clifftop garden, complete with practice green, a rectilinear water feature flows under a walkway and down a series of steps before transforming into a tumbling waterfall that collects in a rock-lined pond.

❺ Filling a confined area with plants means reducing the amount of livable space. Here a compromise has been struck, with plantings contained in garden beds and wall niches.

❶ The aim here was to defer entirely to an overwhelming natural backdrop. Native grasses were planted among large stones at the borders of the deck as a way of anchoring the outdoor living space in its beautifully wild surrounds. A wide awning protects those areas closest to the house, but lower levels have been left fully exposed, providing the opportunity to perch, seemingly out on the edge of the world, as the sun goes down.

❷ A shade house is really nothing more than a cubby house for adults. Building a retreat of some kind into the house itself could not possibly compare with the romantic seclusion offered by this rough-and-ready outbuilding.

❸ The designer of this courtyard made the most of the site's narrow dimensions and steep slope by installing a series of stone steps and surmounting it with an Indian statue from among the owners' collection of Asian artifacts. Designed to have an olfactory impact as well as a visual one, the garden beds were filled with fragrant gardenias, magnolias and orchids. Not immediately apparent among those lush, tropical plantings is a herb garden of thyme, basil, rosemary and parsley, tucked in between the steps.

❶

❶ Building a concrete bench into garden beds acts like a permanent invitation to venture out into a courtyard. Here, it has been made even more inviting with a series of natural-fiber cushions and the addition of a freestanding table and chairs.

❷ This reasonably narrow area has been designed as a series of tailored garden rooms, each one connecting with an internal room. Flooring provides the link: the sandstone paving of the courtyards matches the sandstone flooring of the interior. Clipped hedges and potted topiaries give a furnished feeling to the outdoor spaces. The impression created is that the internal rooms reach all the way out to the back wall of the garden.

❷

❶

INSIDE OUT

The more that an outdoor living space interacts with interior rooms, the more it will be used. Whether that connection is made only visually, via extensive glazing, or spatially, with an enlarged doorway or a retractable wall, depends on issues of climate, space, structural flexibility — and personal preference.

Walls of fixed glazing give internal rooms a feeling of being at one with the outdoors while remaining physically distinct from it, a sensible approach in regions where cold weather predominates for most of the year. If there is scope for more interaction between inside and out, consider installing a wall of glass louvers. Open them, and the sounds and scents of the

❶ The addition of an impressive outdoor fireplace makes this courtyard a space that can be utilized day or night, in warm weather or cool. The floor of the courtyard is almost entirely covered with pavers, a strategy that gives it a very strong, civilized character. A thick planting of tropical species provides enough lush greenery to offset the space's otherwise rather austere finishes.

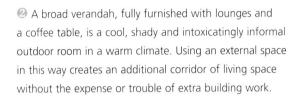

❷ A broad verandah, fully furnished with lounges and a coffee table, is a cool, shady and intoxicatingly informal outdoor room in a warm climate. Using an external space in this way creates an additional corridor of living space without the expense or trouble of extra building work.

❸ Using the same material for the flooring of an internal room and an adjacent external area helps the two spaces to work together as a whole. Wood-framed glass doors allow the internal room to be protected from the weather when necessary without losing the visual link with the outside.

❹ A deep awning offers enough protection from the elements for an outdoor table setting. This deck extends far beyond that sheltered zone, however, making it possible to take full advantage of the sun in cooler weather.

outdoors drift inside; close them, and the room is shut tight against unwanted drafts and chills.

French windows and sliding doors present a wider opening than a standard door and so make more of the connection with the outdoors. With the right structural supports in place, it is possible to install walls that to all intents and purposes can be made to disappear completely. Banks of folding doors are probably the most readily available means of achieving this aim, but with the help of a talented architect you could also develop something more idiosyncratic. For example, you could install a series of wood or glass panels, each of which pivots on a central point, transforming a solid expanse of wall into a series of parallel blades. Or you could opt for huge industrial roller doors and hang them so that they could be pushed back across a windowlesss stretch of wall such as the back wall of a garage, leaving the room completely open to the environment.

❶ Folding glass doors make a literal connection between the internal and external spaces of this house. The canopy window emphasizes the link, making the kitchen and its occupants highly visible from the courtyard.

❷ The broad opening formed by a run of folding doors draws attention away from the low ceiling of the adjacent living area.

❶

❷

❸ Influenced by traditional Asian architecture, this house takes the form of two separate pavilions, linked by a courtyard. The covered walkway provides sheltered passage between the two structures, while the courtyard itself includes informal dining areas and a pool.

❸

❶

❶ A most unusual courtyard makes a special showpiece of this outdoor table setting. The dining platform is surrounded by a pond filled with goldfish. Wooden walkways provide access to the platform from a number of different points within the house.

❷ A series of folding doors makes it possible for this kitchen to open up completely to an internal courtyard. The overhang from the upper story provides permanent shelter for the table setting, which means that it can be used as a casual, al fresco eating area even during a solid downpour or under the punishing midday sun.

❸ Attached to the main body of the house, this elegant wooden gazebo-style structure provides a cool and classic setting for a mid-morning cup of coffee or a festive, lantern-lit gathering on a midsummer's night.

❹ The decision to build a freestanding office at the rear of this site meant that very little outdoor space remained. Rather than leave a token pocket of greenery, it was agreed that the small external space between the house and the office should become a courtyard. The defining feature of the space is a rock wall water feature.

❸ ❹

❶

❶ This indoor–outdoor space runs between the boundary of the property and the front door. Most of the room is covered by a ceiling, but a sloping section of fixed wooden battens provides a permanent, unglazed opening. Basalt stone–clad and concrete walls provide an all-weather finish to the area immediately below that open section. Under cover of the ceiling, those tough materials give way to slightly more refined woods and furnishings.

❷ Taking its cue from classic Italianate architecture, this house incorporates paved spaces that function as external rooms. The pleasingly proportioned archways foster a sense of connection between the internal and external spaces, while reinforcing the substance, solidity and security of the main house. That comforting sense of strength and enclosure need not be lost when pursuing designs that interact with the surrounding environment.

❷

❶

❶ Pavilion formats are becoming increasingly popular in contemporary architecture. By containing particular rooms or groups of rooms in individual structures, the sense of separation between the social spaces and the private pockets of the house is enhanced. Sheltered passageways are a necessary part of the design. Here, a glass-lined corridor stretches across a pond.

❷ This greenhouse room, used for dining, is faced with sliding glass doors that can be pulled back to give the impression that the space is in fact a deep porch or verandah. When the weather is too cold or too hot, the doors can be closed and the airconditioning activated. The extensive glazing and the translucent sheeting material used for the ceiling ensure that the space always feels as though it is part of the garden, even when it is shut tight for optimum temperature control.

❷

SHADE

If you're building from scratch, make sure that outdoor living areas are protected by a canopy of some kind, be it an extension of the roof, a separate fixed awning of a solid material, such as polycarbonate sheeting, or a soft cover of shade cloth. Retractable wall-mounted fabric awnings can be used to shade courtyards adjacent to the house, but living areas located at some distance from the main building require a free-standing shade structure.

The simplest solution might be to let your landscaping provide the shade: a towering oak, for example, makes a wonderful living canopy. Almost as easy is the installation of a pergola covered by a climbing plant — evergreen in warm climates, deciduous in cooler areas.

Gazebos, cabanas and pagodas — shade houses of all kinds — can be used to make an outdoor space substantially more livable. In practical terms, they provide shelter from wind, rain and hot sun, but they also invite you into the garden, encouraging you to be a participant, not just a spectator. These freestanding garden rooms can also be used to increase the amount of living space in the house, serving as a guest bedroom, a children's playroom or a home office. Some areas may have restrictions on the size of structure that can be erected in a garden and on its use; check with local authorities before embarking on any building.

❶ Verandahs play a crucial role in hot-climate architecture. Clearly, they provide a pleasantly shaded area for outdoor living, but they also keep sunlight from falling directly on the walls and create a belt of cooled air that wraps around the house.

❶

❷ ❸
❹ ❺

❷ A roof of polycarbonate sheeting casts a light shade over this area without sealing it off entirely from the blue skies above.

❸ Antique Balinese statues and doors feature in the construction of this poolside cabana.

❹ Modeled on a traditional tea house, this structure is the literal and metaphorical high point of a Japanese garden on a steeply sloping block.

❺ A vine-covered pergola and a hammock represent minimal construction yet they clearly form an attractive, beguiling and very livable outdoor space.

❶ A shade cloth is a practical way of introducing a shade element to an existing structure without the fuss or expense of building work. It can also be quite unobtrusive, as is the case here — the white cloth scarcely registers against the pale exterior walls.

❷ Protection from the sun is essential, even in the mildest of climates. A solid shade structure may not be necessary, but an outdoor table setting must at least be sheltered by an umbrella.

❸ Shade cloths can provide good protection from ultra-violet radiation, yet their visual impact on an outdoor space is minimal.

❶

❶ Modern market-style umbrellas designed for outdoor use have superior durability and can weather harsh sunlight and extended periods of rain. They also come in a range of large sizes and can function like a gazebo without walls.

❷ More than a gazebo, this structure is an independent entertainment pavilion. Separated from the house by a lavish tropical garden, it provides a venue for social occasions, both formal and informal, and keeps the associated noise and bustle away from the more private living spaces.

❷

GROUND COVERINGS

Grass can be used as the "floor" of an outdoor living space, but it must be a species that wears well, that can cope with a certain amount of shade and that doesn't die away in cold weather. Grass makes for a soft and luxuriant surface, but it needs regular watering and mowing, so it's probably best avoided if you plan to have extensive furniture settings.

Hard surfaces are a very reliable alternative, being both hard-wearing and easy to maintain. Basic concrete pavers do the job well and are relatively inexpensive. Search out colored pavers or aggregate pavers that incorporate flecks of marble, shell or glass if you want a more interesting surface.

❶ Flagstones create a solid and stable surface that can withstand the wear and tear of regular outdoor entertaining.

❷ A hard floor gives an outdoor space a roomlike character and reinforces its role as an alternative living space.

❸ Gravel surfaces are a traditional treatment in French gardens and provide a deliciously satisfying crunch underfoot. They are best kept to areas located at a distance from the house, however, as the small particles can cause damage to carpets or wooden floors.

Bricks and terra-cotta tiles can both be used to great effect in an indoor–outdoor area. As a hard surface, they provide a practical platform for furniture, but their organic tones blend in comfortably with surrounding garden areas. Terra cotta is an absorbent material that will stain, and while the patina of age can be very appealing, the greasy smudges around a barbecue are most definitely not. If you plan to use terra cotta in an area where it will be susceptible to stains, be sure to have the tiles treated with a sealant.

Pebbles and gravel also look at home in an outdoor setting. They are extremely easy to lay, but the area must be edged to ensure that the stones don't invade nearby lawn, garden beds or internal living areas. Both pebbles and gravel are very traditional surfaces for outdoor spaces — think of the gravel pathways of a French garden or the pebble mosaic courtyards of Moorish architecture. They can, however, look sleek and modern, especially if used in combination with concrete slabs.

Wooden decking offers several advantages. Built as a platform of planks that rest on joists, it can be installed even where the ground is sloping. Instead of leveling the land, as you would to lay tiles or stone, it's a relatively fuss-free matter of using supports of varying height underneath the wood to even up the surface, rather like the foundations of a house. A deck leading from the house is a common sight, but wood can also be installed as a free-standing platform, perhaps within the hedges of a "secret garden" or built around the trunk of a gracious shade tree.

❶ Wood is a conservative choice as a ground cover and will not compete with the garden for attention. Installed as a conventional deck, it will provide a reliable surface for outdoor furniture while making minimum visual impact on its surroundings.

❶

❷ This courtyard has the hard surfaces and solid shade structures that make an outdoor area permanently useful as a living space, yet it still has the untrammeled charm of a country garden. The trick has been to soften those surfaces with plants. Various climbers clad the walls and the pergola while the paving stones are surrounded by mini mondo grass.   ❷

❶ Being merely an adjunct to a serious swimmer's pool located elsewhere on the property, this so-called "jungle pool" was designed for pure recreation.

❷ This guest cabana has a pool quite literally at its doorstep. At night, the sound of water trickling from spouts below the potted plants creates a soothing atmosphere.

❷

❸

❸ Plantings around a pool must be able to cope with extreme conditions. They will usually be in full sunlight for a large part of the day and they will be exposed to salt, chlorine and chemicals.

❶

POOLS

An in-ground swimming pool can be a tremendous asset to a house. Whether it is used for swimming laps, cooling off or keeping the kids rapturously busy in vacation times, it makes for a fabulous family resource. It can also be a lot of trouble. Pools take time and money to maintain. What's more, a pool that has turned green with neglect is an embarrassing eyesore and a waste of garden space. Only commit to the large cost of installing an in-ground pool if you are confident that you and your family will be able and willing to keep it in good order.

Given the high cost of installation and maintenance, it seems a shame to let the pool go to waste for six months or more out of every year. Relatively speaking, a heating system will not add that much to the initial outlay. The least expensive option is a cover or blanket that lies on the surface of the water, trapping heat. Ease of installation and comparatively low price can make this option appealing, especially for a pre-existing pool, but the temperature gains are modest and you may still find the pool water too cold for comfort through the winter months and perhaps even into late fall and early spring. Electric and solar-powered systems cost more, but can raise temperatures to a very comfortable level, making the pool fully functional all year round.

① Proof of how a lap pool can be installed in the slimmest of sites, this example was built into a verandah on the side of the house that faces the sun.

② This tiny pool takes up next to no space, yet it gives the owners the luxury of taking an icy plunge on a hot day. The moving water of the waterfall feature on the rear wall alleviates the sense of enclosure.

②

Over the years, pools have been common inclusions in rambling family houses and lavishly appointed mansions, but rarely seen in homes where space is less abundant. Recently, though, a couple of space-saving pool designs have emerged and been adopted with enthusiasm by city-dwellers. Where the space is really cramped, you can install a jet pool measuring just a few yards (meters) square. The submerged water jets pump out water at varying velocities. Set the jets to a low speed and walk against the current for a gentle, low-impact form of exercise, or turn them up and swim with as much pace as you would in a full-size pool. In a long, narrow space, you can opt for a lap pool. Most lap pools look like a thin slice of a full-size pool, measuring one or two swimming lanes in width and 15 or 25 yards or meters in length.

③ The pool itself is a simple, straight-lined model, but the finishes imbue it with a sense of opulence. The interior is clad in blue mosaic tiles while the surrounds are covered with sandstone. Of course, the area's focal point is an elaborate wooden shade house that can also serve as guest quarters.

③

❶ In search of privacy, the owners decided
to install this pool at the side of the house
away from the living spaces. Padded benches
and a crowd of cushions offer home comforts
away from the house itself.

❷ Inspired by the lavish swimming pools
of island resorts, this pool was designed as
an oasis in the suburbs. A small mound of
natural rocks build up the far corner, creating
a waterfall and providing a bed for plantings
of palms and ferns. Other rocks are installed
in the pool itself, mounted on shallow underwater shelves, where bathers can recline and
children can frolic.

❸

❸ Designed with a South Pacific feeling, this
outdoor area combines streamlined built
structures with showy tropical plantings, a
teaming of contrasts that delivers a fresh
exuberance to the space. A spa sits at the
end of a long, slim lap pool, separated from
it by a short stretch of paving and matching
the neat dimensions of the larger body of
water. The blue tiles that clad the interior
of both the pool and the spa are responsible
for the water's dazzling color.

❷

❸

WATER FEATURES

A water feature, be it graceful and traditional or sculptural and modern, can become the focal point of a garden or a courtyard, but it has functional benefits, too. The sound of trickling water can be a calming, even lulling, influence. As gentle as it is, it can drown out the squeals of children, the drone of traffic or the blare of a television, simply by providing an aural distraction.

Basic ponds and some of the more simple fountains and water spouts are often sold in kit form and can be assembled by a nonprofessional. Any project that requires sophisticated plumbing and electrical skills should be handled by an expert, not only for safety's sake but also to avoid the complications of water damage that can result from a botched installation.

Any body of water measuring 1 foot (30 cm) or more in depth is a drowning risk. If you have small children and want a risk-free water feature, you could install a water spout, assembling it so that the water flows into a below-ground reservoir rather than an open pool or pond. The reservoir, which will contain both the water and the pump, should be covered with a wire grille. This mesh can then be covered with pebbles that hide the reservoir and the grille, and create a splashing surface for the tumbling water.

Apartment dwellers need not go without a water feature. Even a balcony offers room enough for the installation of a wall-mounted water spout. These are self-contained plaques comprising a spout and a bowl. The water that falls into the bowl is pumped back up to the spout to fall again.

❶ Stepping stones laid in an even, geometric pattern are present more for graphic effect than for practical reasons, although they do provide access to the espaliered pear tree for maintenance.

❶

❷ Influenced by southeast Asian architecture, this house of free-standing pavilions uses waterways as an alternative to solid garden landscaping. The result is decidedly exotic, but relies on thorough planning and perfectly executed construction; anything less, and the stability of the built structures could be seriously undermined.

❷

❶

❷

❶ Water features bring life to a garden. They are an obvious home for fish, but they also attract birds and insects. Even the sound of lapping or trickling water can introduce a gentle dynamic to a garden space.

❷ Steel beams, usually employed as building materials, are installed here as water chutes. The water tumbles into a box-shaped spa which, with its rocky setting, decorative finishes and innovative construction, presents as a water feature when not in use. The body of water in the foreground is a goldfish pond filled with water lilies and umbrella cyperus.

③

④

③ This decorative pond separates an outdoor entertaining area from a nearby pool with surrounding courtyard. Stepping stones across the surface of the pond provide passage between the two spaces.

④ Water trickles from three outlets spaced across the surface of this pebble wall, collecting in a below-ground reservoir before being pumped back up to the outlets again. The reservoir is covered by a steel grille which itself is overlaid with pebbles, ensuring that the water feature is not a safety hazard.

❶

❶ Formal landscaping relies on balance for its sense of calm and restraint. Here, a pair of urns at either end of the pool enhances the symmetrical composition of the space.

❷ Lion's-head spouts are a classic element of water features and a handsome component of a formal garden space. A pump located within the pond feeds the water back up to the spouts to keep the feature flowing.

②

③ Designed to look like a natural waterfall, this feature provides a link between the two levels of a clifftop garden. The pond in which the water collects is located beside a swimming pool, creating the illusion that the pool is fed by the waterfall.

④ Talk of water features sometimes conjures images of classical statuary and ornate fountains, but, as this example shows, they can have a markedly contemporary identity. In this instance, red mosaic tiles clad a rectilinear pond and a feature wall. A spout delivers a continuous sheet of water that has a suitably graphic impact.

③ ④

LIGHTING

A thoughtfully lit garden can be a magical environment.
The key is to err on the side of restraint while still providing
adequate task lighting. Paths, for example, should be clearly
lit. A movement-activated floodlight, harsh but functional, is
a satisfactory solution, but a more elegant alternative would be
to install a series of lights along the edges of the path. These
could be set into the paving material itself, or in the adjacent
garden. Choose light fittings that cast light down onto or
across the path rather than up into the face of those using it.
Solar-powered light fittings come into their own in a garden
setting, absorbing light energy during the day and emitting a
gentle glow after dark.

Dining and seating areas, too, must have a reasonable amount
of light. Wall-mounted uplights or downlights will supply
an adequate amount of illumination. Lights could also be
installed along the boundary wall at foot level, creating a glow
around the periphery that helps to define the space while
providing enough light for safe and comfortable use of the area.

A swimming pool can be a dead zone when
not in use, taking up a large amount of
garden space yet contributing nothing to the
atmosphere of the property. Lights fitted into
the surface of the pool mean that it can be
used at night, but, perhaps more importantly,
they have the power to turn a recreational
space into an atmospheric water feature.

Once the task lighting is in place, you can start thinking about the more atmospheric aspects of the garden lighting scheme: a floodlight for the illumination of a majestic elm, sparkling fairylights dotting a hedge or moody underwater lights in a pond.

Electricity must be handled with great care outdoors. Cables need to be laid deep enough that they won't be accidentally dug up or carelessly cut through with a shovel, and they must be protected from moisture. You must leave this job to a qualified electrician.

❶ During the day, the vivid blue tiles that line this stream emphasize the geometry of the feature. At night, uplights at the base of each urn play up the sense of majestic passage down the length of the stream to the illuminated water jet in the pond.

❷ Capped fittings cast light down on the floor area of this courtyard, but avoid throwing glare up into the faces of those using the area.

❸ A motion-activated floodlight is a safe and energy-efficient way to illuminate pathways, but cannot be expected to provide anything in the way of atmosphere.

❶ This lighting scheme is proof of how safety requirements can be met without any loss of style. Capped fittings installed inconspicuously in the fronts of the bench seats cast light on the paved floor of the courtyard, while a dramatic wall light illuminates the entrance area. The double-height, segmented expanse of glazing that faces a stairwell also plays a role in illuminating the outdoor area.

❷ Feature lighting ensures that decorative elements, such as these Asian clay tigers, don't go missing after dark. Often, the shadows cast by this sort of lighting are as influential as the sculptural pieces themselves, creating an exotic and mildly mischievous mood.

❸ Adequate illumination of stairs and pathways is essential if they are to be used safely after dark. The chic metal surrounds of these recessed stair lights and their decisive, symmetrical installation pattern turn a functional necessity into a defining design element.

❶

9

perfect

COLOR

In a matter of hours, a tin of raincoat yellow, princess pink or dark chocolate paint can transform a bedroom into sunny playground, teen paradise or moody adult domain for a hundred dollars or less. No other design tool offers quite such good value, nor so much versatility. Lose your color inhibitions and discover a wealth of decorating possibilities and finely tuned aesthetic control.

PREVIOUS PAGES Small doses of color can have a surprisingly big impact. Here, a dash of scarlet on a wall and a paint-box set of dining chairs make these spaces stand out.

❶ Even an artful arrangement of little glazed feature tiles can lift a somber-toned wall.

❷ When choosing exterior colors, consider the palette of the surrounding landscape.

❶

❷

❸ If you're not confident with color, start by introducing some contrasting tones in the form of freestanding furniture pieces. Keeping the architectural shell neutral is also a safe approach if you're thinking of reselling the property in the near future.

PERFECT COLOR

You could do far worse than walk into a new house and paint it all white: every wall, banister, cabinet front and window frame. An all-white interior is both serene and sensible. White instantly unifies every room in the house from end to end and top to bottom. It doesn't challenge the eye. It doesn't distract attention from furniture pieces or artworks. And it can always be enlivened with a dash of color from a simple bowl of green apples, a vase brimming with sepia-toned dahlias or a seasonal swap of accessories, such as mossy green and chocolate bed linen and blankets in winter or lantern-bright red, pink and orange tableware in summer.

But while white is probably most valued for what it doesn't do, color is treasured for the active role it takes in an interior. It can establish the tone of a house and enhance the moods of its occupants. And it has a crafty capacity to emphasize and conceal the assets and liabilities of a space, drawing focus to a glorious view or a glamorous staircase, disguising the awkwardness of a room formed by five or six walls of unequal length, creating an impression of height in a room with a low ceiling and bringing together the interior and exterior spaces of a townhouse and courtyard.

Having acknowledged the power of color, the challenge remains to decide upon the colors that best suit you, your house, your environment and your style of living. Remember, though, that the colors you use in your house will physically surround you, becoming your very environment. For that reason, you need to think about colors in terms of how they make you feel, not just your visual impression of them. You might like the look of a jungle-green Versace dress, but that doesn't necessarily mean you would feel comfortable living in a room of that color.

INSTINCT AND INSPIRATION

If you're lucky, your intuition will guide you and make clear the associations between a given color and the emotional response it arouses in you. It's common, though, to feel your instincts undermined by the sheer number and scope of the colors available. To get back in touch with those instincts, leaf through some old decorating magazines and books, tearing out or tagging those rooms and color schemes that appeal to you. After a while, a pattern should emerge, giving you a clear idea of the colors to which you are drawn and reinforcing your perhaps shaky hunches about your own personal style.

Those images are also likely to suggest multihued color schemes, but don't worry if none of them appeals — the sources of inspiration are everywhere when it comes to mixing and matching shades. Nowhere do colors appear in more intriguing, more gratifying or more harmonious combinations than in nature. The palettes presented are various and sometimes surprisingly sophisticated, from the refined silver-gray, parchment and vivid rust of an aged piece of bark or the modulating blue and blue-green tones of the ocean, to the unfettered vibrance of exotic birds, the dramatic ebony and tangerine of glowing embers or the fresh and lively clash of crimson pink and mouth-watering green in a slice of watermelon.

❶ A muted red reminiscent of antique lacquerware evokes images of the decadent and mysteriously sophisticated Oriental interiors of 1930s crime novels and Bond-girl boudoirs. A trio of beachy neutrals tones down the more extravagant notes of the shade, resulting in a scheme that is exotic but refined and restrained.

❷ Blue and orange, colors poised on opposite sides of the color wheel, make a classic and inherently dynamic combination. When the bright-hued primary versions of the colors are not in vogue, the dulled-down denim blue and the earthy terra-cotta shades sit comfortably in contemporary spaces.

❸ Shades of grape and plum carry some of the luscious appeal of other fruit-inspired tones, such as strawberry and watermelon, but in a more serious, more sensual vein. An accent of super-cool gray ensures that their fruitier tendencies are kept in check.

❹ Selecting colors that lie close together on the color wheel is a sure way of imbuing a space — or a series of spaces — with calm, consistent confidence. Remember, though, that the colors should have a similar tone. Teaming a grass green with an army green will yield an uneven, uncomfortable result, but a combination of muted shades, such as pea green, fir green, forest floor and bleached khaki, will be a success.

Global cultures, too, offer tried and true color combinations, forged by the local environment and seen out by generations over hundreds, even thousands, of years. The startling white and luminous blue of the Greek islands is a classic example, but there are many others, such as the raw linen and dull red of rural France, the recurrent pink and indigo of India, the sun-drenched ochers and sea-kissed turquoise of Mexico.

Even the un-natural world — the world of human activity and manufacture — can be a source of inspiration for color combinations. The pattern in a scrap of vintage fabric, the watercolors in a long-admired painting, the jaunty glazes of a collection of eggcups, bright red buses on a gray city street or the eye-catching label on a tin of tomatoes — any of these could be the starting point for a clever and distinctive scheme.

An earthy, organic red is the dominant feature of this living area. It gives this space a sense of warmth and drama even when there is no flame in the fireplace.

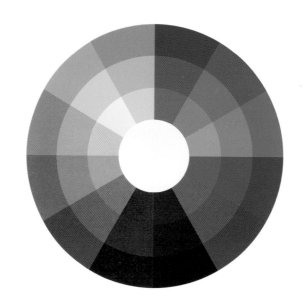

The schoolbook connotations of the color wheel tend to daunt some people, yet it is invaluable as a starting point for creative color combinations. Select colors from around the wheel in analogous, complementary or complex combinations for schemes that are either subtle or dynamic. The best outcomes are achieved when all color choices lie within the same band of intensity.

COMBINING COLORS

If the overwhelming possibilities of color combinations have clouded your judgment, returning to the basics can be a worthwhile exercise. In technical terms, there are essentially four foolproof strategies.

The simplest of all is the monochrome color scheme. It's not quite as limiting as it sounds: rather than using a single hue on every wall, cushion, lampshade and tabletop, it's a matter of layering a number of shades throughout the space. Imagine a deliciously plump sofa with lavender blue loose covers scattered with serge and navy blue cushions in a room where the walls are painted a delicate ice blue. Even with such variations in tone, a monochromatic scheme can be somewhat under-stimulating. Prints, patterns and textured finishes can save the simple scheme from lapsing into dullness.

Slightly more sophisticated is the analogous color scheme, utilizing three or four shades that lie alongside each other on the color wheel. The variations between these shades can be quite minimal, but, for the sake of illustrating the point, think of a scheme that includes yellow, lime and green, or green, turquoise and blue.

❶

❶ Wood stains are a different way of introducing chromatic diversity. Here, panels have been stained within a palette that runs from ocher through rust to plum.

❷ Earthy shades achieve a warm neutrality, making it possible to enjoy the soothing simplicity of a modern bedroom without resorting to the cool and clinical look of some contemporary styled spaces.

❸ White walls tend to focus attention on the contents of a room, a device that can be very serviceable when there is a stunning work of art or an extraordinary piece of furniture to be featured. Walls in a suitable shade of off-white or cream, on the other hand, allow the individual pieces to recede, creating a comfortable, soft-edged space suitable for relaxed living.

❷

❸

These combinations work because all colors in the series are the same "temperature" — being either warm colors or cool colors — and because they all share one underlying hue. In the case of the first example, yellow is the constant; in the second, it is blue. These strong connections ensure a sense of harmony.

If you're looking for more dynamism in a color scheme, consider the complementary combinations. These are made up of colors that lie directly opposite each other on the color wheel, such as navy and burnt umber, fuchsia pink and bud green, or eggplant and chartreuse. These pairings have instant appeal, but remember that they are naturally stimulating, a characteristic that might make for a wonderful choice in a family room or a children's playroom but is best avoided in a bedroom.

Complex combinations deal with colors located at equal intervals around the color wheel. Complex trios include terra cotta, chartreuse and lavender, or saffron, turquoise and plum. A complex quartet might be rose pink, leaf green, lavender and butternut. Using so many colors can result in a scheme of satisfying depth and diversity, but it does require deft handling and so is best left to experienced decorators.

Whichever approach you choose, allow one color to dominate. When colors are equally prominent, they tend to vie for attention, keeping the eye flicking from one surface to the next and undermining any sense of composure. Instead, stagger the proportions, letting one color take the lead and a second perform a supporting role. Additional colors should appear as accents only.

❶

❶ Using a range of colors throughout a house can give a wonderful vitality to the interior. The secret is to work with shades of a similar intensity. Here, a picture-book blue, a dewy shade of peach and a sublime yellow achieve a sort of youthful naivety, a whimsical contrast to the pared-back architectural form.

❷ Cutaways in the blue wall of a staircase provide glimpses of the color schemes in adjacent spaces. In combination with artful display niches, the cutaways have all the visual interest of framed artworks.

❸ Color is one of the least expensive design tools available. This is apparent here, in the case of standard glazed tiles. Cornflower blue tiles don't cost any more than plain old white ones, and using them in combination can charge a room with style.

❷

❸

Varying colors from room to room can energize a house, giving it a refreshing sense of movement, openness and personality. A truly wild and bohemian household might get away with using completely unrelated colors from one room to another, the very unorthodoxy of the approach adding up to something appropriately gregarious and raffish. In more conservative households, however, it pays to adhere to certain restraints.

A coherent outcome is most easily achieved when all colors are of the same intensity. Intensity refers to the purity of a tone, for example a brick red is clearly a duller shade than a fire-engine red, a khaki is duller than a grassy green and so on. Maintaining a consistent intensity gives you the freedom to use multiple colors throughout the house; for example, petal pink, butter-cup yellow and bud green would look sweet in each of the three bedrooms of a wooden cottage, while a dark stormy blue, a gunmetal gray and a pea green could be a handsome treatment for, respectively, the dining room, study and living room of a city apartment.

❶

❶ A consistent level of chromatic intensity is evident throughout the interior spaces of this house. Even the dark-brown leather of the sofa has a cool tone, in keeping with the restrained shades used on the walls.

❷ Broad stripes are a strong statement on this soaring ceiling and have the effect of making those upper reaches seem much closer than they really are. As a result, this living space benefits from an enormous amount of natural light without losing its sense of intimacy.

❸ Reds and oranges make for a vibrant interior well suited to a living space that is often used for entertaining.

❷

❸

THE RULES

Whatever your favorite hues, and whatever combinations you intend to use them in, there are certain principles that hold true in any circumstance.

Possibly the best known of these is that warm colors make a large room seem smaller and cool colors make a small room seem larger: imagine harvest gold in a sprawling living room or baby blue in a tiny bedroom. This effect can be explained beyond question by science, but in essence it comes down to the relative wavelengths of the colors at either end of the spectrum and how they move through space, with the result that warm tones literally reach the eye sooner and thus give the impression that they are advancing, drawing surfaces nearer than they really are.

One important thing to realize is that ostensibly cool colors, such as blue, can be warmed up by adding some warm tones to the blend, and vice versa. That means that a large or sparsely furnished room can be made more cozy by, say, a rich berry blue or a pewter-toned gray and that a pale lime-toned yellow can give some breathing space to a cramped kitchen.

The same sorts of principles hold true for sun-filled rooms (those that face south in the Northern hemisphere and north in the Southern hemisphere) and shadowy rooms (north-facing

The use of a warm, earthy shade successfully makes this sprawling open-plan space seem more cozy. A contrasting denim tone clearly distinguishes these recreational spaces from the workspace of the kitchen beyond.

in the Northern hemisphere, south-facing in the Southern).
In the absence of direct light, the light in sunless spaces tends
to be cool, meaning that a pure white wall would have a bluish
cast. Conversely, a stark white wall in a sunlit room would
have a yellow-orange tone to it. Where these characteristics
are evident in the extreme — that is, in a room that receives
absolutely no sunshine or in one that is flooded with sunlight
to an uncomfortable level — it's advisable to decorate with
colors that counteract these conditions, using warm colors
in the shady rooms and cool ones in the sunny rooms.

It's worth remembering at this point that a basically "white"
room can be rendered in any one of an extraordinary range
of tints. One American paint manufacturer claims a range of
whites that numbers into the hundreds. Sometimes the active
tint in these colored whites is easily identifiable, such as in the
most preciously fragile of pale pinks or the very crispest and
palest of pale greens. In other instances, however, the tint is
scarcely discernible. These hues can be extremely valuable in
balancing the cool or warm tendencies of the light in different
rooms. Handled well, they can result in a room that looks as
flawlessly and purely white as any art-gallery wall.

Color can also be called into service to overcome awkward
dimensions. For example, the narrowness of a long, thin
room can be countered by painting one of the shorter ends
in a warm hue such as an earthy terra cotta, a regal purple
or an attention-grabbing scarlet. The warm tone will trick
the subconscious into thinking that the surface is closer than
it really is, thus "shortening" the gangly longer walls. Ceiling
height can be manipulated in a similar manner, especially if
the room has a picture rail running around the walls. Use
a darker tone above the picture rail than below it to make
the ceiling seem to sit more snugly. Do the reverse, and an
oppressively low ceiling will be given a lift.

❶ This mild rawhide tone succeeds as a feature wall in a small, poorly lit bedroom because it is neither too cool nor too vivid. In fact, it almost functions as a neutral, a chromatic extension of the wooden floor.

❶

❷ | ❸
❹ | ❺

❷ Cool whites are a suitable match for the austere surfaces of this chic contemporary room and help keep it feeling fresh in hot weather. One block of color, in the form of a mustard-yellow lounge, lifts the whole space.

❸ In a conservatively finished interior, art can be used to introduce an element of color.

❹ Rich, jewel-like shades have been used throughout history to establish an opulent atmosphere in formal interiors. They also contribute a visual warmth, which can be valuable in a cold climate.

❺ A nutty olive shade is cool enough to counter the stultifying heat of the summer sun in this family living area.

10

FUNDAMENTALS

Floors, doors, windows and passageways don't only give physical form to a space, they also affect the volume and character of light, the acoustic privacy and thermal comfort in a room, the ease of accessibility and the temperature and flow of air. Hugely influential in creating the atmosphere of a room, these structural components are an underestimated ally in the quest for the perfect home.

WINDOWS

The enormous strategic value of windows is often overlooked. Choose the right ones and position them well and they will not only give the exterior of your house a pleasing appearance, they will also go a long way toward creating the ambiance of the living areas within. The shape and the orientation of the windows determine the volume and even the quality of light inside the house and can make the difference between an airless room and a well-ventilated one.

As a starting point, make sure the glazed area of the windows is equal to at least 10 percent of the total floor area; that figure will provide an absolute minimum of illumination, but enough to make a room technically "livable." If refurbishing, try to maintain the visual rhythm that is already established by keeping distances between windows regular and by making an effort to line up the top and bottom of each new window with those already in place. If the windows are different shapes and sizes, stick to a central axis point by lining up all the top edges or all the bottom edges or by running an invisible line through the midpoint of every frame.

PREVIOUS PAGES Floors, walls, doors, windows and staircases set the tone of a room as powerfully as any furnishings. Here, open staircases and robust floors suggest an interior ready for the rough and tumble of a youthful but style-conscious household.

❶ The external walls of this living space are almost entirely composed of glazing. Because of this, the space seems to mesh with the surrounding garden even in the cooler months, when windows and doors are shut tight.

① This striking home folds around three sides of a swimming pool. Doors from the kitchen provide access, while a fixed panel of glass furnishes the dining area with views of the pool without the noise, traffic and splashes of a working opening. A louvered slot window is positioned to promote cross ventilation.

② Folding windows in a corner enable a bench seat to be transformed into a garden seat.

②

It's also very important to consider where you site your windows, remembering that east-facing windows will catch the gentle morning light and west-facing windows the harsh light of the setting sun. In the Northern hemisphere, south-facing windows will draw in light for the largest part of the day, while those that face due north will not receive any direct light. The opposite is true for the Southern hemisphere. Windows that receive no direct sun still have a role to play, however. In built-up areas they can let in a surprising volume of indirect light reflected off surrounding buildings and they can also prove useful in promoting cross ventilation through a room. In a warm climate, a window positioned low on a sunless wall will draw in cool air from the shaded side of the house. As the fresh air moves in, the warm air that has gathered inside the house will naturally drift out of any open windows located high on any of the other walls.

③ Fixed panels of glass set high on the wall toward the ceiling admit an enormous amount of natural light, without compromising the privacy of the interior in a built-up area.   ③

❶ Panels of glass replace walls and ceiling in a conservatory-style extension. The structure of the room creates a sunlit interior of surprising warmth, even in the cold winter months. Such an extensive use of glazing could not be recommended in hot climates.

❶

❷ Walls of windows that look out across a lake manipulate the impression of space in what is quite a small kitchen and family dining room. Look closely and you will see that there is only limited floorspace around the eating table and the island, yet it is the far horizon, not the masonry wall, that seems to define the boundaries of the space.

❷

WINDOW STYLES

As the name suggests, fixed-pane windows are fixed panels of glazing within a frame of wood or aluminum set directly into the framework or brickwork of a building. A fixed window can be particularly useful in situations where there is a need for light, but when the window will be seldom opened due to noise problems or security risks or because it will be installed high up on a wall and out of reach. It can also be useful in coastal areas where views and sunshine are desirable, but the onslaught of strong sea breezes is not. Remember, too, that fixed windows don't have to be square or rectangular; they can be arched, circular, triangular or hexagonal — the possibilities are limited only by the abilities of your supplier.

Sash windows — also known as box-frame or double-hung windows — will be familiar to anyone who has ever spent time in a 19th-century row house or cottage. Traditionally, these were made with wooden frames that slid up and down with the aid of weighted ropes or sashes. Today, the weights and sashes have been replaced with sprung fittings and the frames can be made in low-maintenance aluminum. Many sash windows in older houses have seen so many coats of paint that one or other of the panels has become fixed into position. When in good working order, however, the panels should both move freely, giving you the option of having the opening at either the upper or lower half of the window. This can be useful in a dining room, for example, where you might want to avoid having breezes passing through at table height. One thing to keep in mind is that the open portion of a sash window will only ever equal half the total area of the window. In that respect, it is not as spatially efficient as a louvered window for promoting ventilation. In cooler climates, this hardly matters, but in tropical and subtropical environments it can be an issue of some significance.

There are two types of hinged windows: casement windows, with hinges on one of the two vertical sides, and awning or canopy windows, with hinges at either the top or bottom. Casement windows swing out horizontally; awning windows swing either up or down. Traditionally, these windows were held open by a rod, a series of holes in the rod representing the different widths to which the window could be opened. Modern models usually have a built-in winding mechanism. Many also incorporate a key-operated lock so that the window opening can be securely set at different widths.

Louvered windows are composed of pivoting slats of glass, usually set into an aluminum frame. A lever operation alters the angle of the blades from the upright, closed position to the fully open, horizontal position and everything in between. This flexibility represents excellent control, making it possible to direct breezes toward the ceiling away from a sleeping baby, or across to a lounge area where adults are sitting. When fully open, the louvered window offers an airflow of close to 100 percent of the available opening, a property that makes it an extremely effective tool of ventilation in warmer climates. In the past, louvered windows presented a security risk because intending intruders could easily slide out individual panels of glazing and slip through the opening. Modern louvered windows are more tamper resistant and can even be made with security bars running through the center of each slat.

❶ Fixed glass panels increase the volume of light in an extension at the rear of a worker's cottage. The panels are deployed in a graphic pattern to match the sculptural quality of the rest of the interior. One panel features louvers that can be left open to allow the hot, moist air produced in the kitchen to waft outside.

❶

❷ In a house overlooking a well-used waterway, a series of sliding glass doors maximizes the possibility of light penetration, strong air flow and enviable views. Wooden shutters on the far edge of the balcony area are used to control light levels, to shelter the indoor and outdoor spaces from rain and unpleasant winds and to maintain privacy.

❷

GLAZING

Different types of glass and glazing treatments make it possible to use any window style in virtually any set of circumstances. In a noisy environment by a main road or near an airport, a window frame can be fitted with double glazing. This consists of two parallel panes of glass forming an air lock that makes a dramatic difference to sound penetration. In a bathroom or stairwell — both places where accidents can easily occur — windows can be fitted with toughened or safety glass. And in any area where privacy is an issue, sandblasted, etched or frosted glass can be used instead of conventional clear glass.

Colored, patterned and textured glazing tends to be thought of in association with period homes — and indeed many suppliers specialize in products that can be used in restoration work — but such types of glass can be used to great effect in contemporary houses, too. While ripple-finish Arctic glass might be seen in the bathroom windows of early 20th-century homes, decoratively slubbed and bubbled art glass could form a partition wall in a modern house, perhaps between a bedroom and an adjoining bathroom. And while ruby-red and sapphire-blue glass panels might appear as insets in entry doors in Victorian homes, pure white milk glass could be used in a door frame in a modern house, letting in plenty of light yet still providing a degree of privacy.

Proximity to a neighboring property meant that privacy was a problematic issue for this open-plan refurbishment. The solution was to use fixed panels of frosted glass that would give a filtered flow of light without exposing the interior of the house.

❶ A wall of very sophisticated glazing fronts this house. The rhythmic pattern of frames contains a combination of sliding doors and fixed glass panels, as well as frameless vertical sliding windows. The interior frames are faced with wood, in keeping with the house's organic, minimalist aesthetic, but the exterior is composed of all-weather aluminum in a sleek, silver, anodized finish.

❷ Stairwells that rest against an external wall can make the most of their location with the addition of windows. Here, a long, vertical line of fixed glass panels illuminates this important traffic zone. At night, when lit, it also contributes to the attractive geometry of the external courtyard.

❸ Windows fitted with folding doors break down the boundaries between internal and external spaces. This wide opening poised on a corner of an open-plan living and kitchen area invites fresh air and healthful sunlight into the interior. It also makes the facilities of the kitchen readily accessible to anyone using the courtyard.

❶

❷

❸

DOORS

Doors can take up a surprising amount of floorspace, a factor that must be considered in the planning stages of new building work. Hinged doors are the most space hungry, requiring a sweep of floor area as well as a section of free wall space comparable to the size of the door itself to accommodate the door when it is fully open. A conventional sliding door requires a similar amount of wall space, but obviously will not require room to be swung open. An expensive but extremely attractive and streamlined option is to install doors that slide back into a wall cavity, so that wall space on either side can be fully utilized for furniture placement or the display of artwork. Folding doors can be used across broad openings, even in the place of whole walls. They can provide excellent flexibility when installed internally, easily closing off a kitchen in a compact open-plan living area, or creating a generous play area when fitted between two children's bedrooms. Externally, they can be used to radically expose the interior of the house to the outside world. A fully retracted length of folding doors transforms an internal living room and an external courtyard into one vast indoor–outdoor area, ideal for active families or for entertaining on a large scale.

Folding doors can give a space an enormous amount of flexibility, as this room illustrates. When these doors are fully retracted, an external stone feature wall becomes the outer boundary of this living room, effectively increasing the floorspace to include a narrow strip of decking. This long, thin external space running down one side of the building has little functional value on its own, but its potential is realized when it becomes part of the interior living space.

❶

❷

❶ Track-mounted, steel-framed doors have a streamlined industrial look well suited to this sleek warehouse conversion. The glass panels allow the space to benefit from the natural light entering the building through windows on a far wall. Lower panels are frosted to protect privacy in the bathroom, but the upper panels are clear, retaining the sightlines that reveal the impressive dimensions of an unusual architectural shell.

❷ Eternally popular, french doors have a classic look that makes them compatible with many different styles of period home. Their glass-paneled construction means that interiors benefit from light penetration even when the doors are closed. Their fine frames and inherent symmetry naturally impart a refined and graceful air.

③

④

③ An oversized door is a generous gesture at the entrance to a house, the structural embodiment of wide-open arms. It is also surprisingly practical, making it easy to move large pieces of furniture in and out of the house as well as improving access for people with disabilities.

④ An industrial roller door replaces a wall in this extraordinary rural house. The conversion of a rustic barn forms the basis of the building. The scale of the roller door is a good match for the soaring proportions of the barn, but it also contributes to the edgy, contemporary, urban aesthetic evident throughout the house. When the weather is warm and the door retracted, the interior is completely exposed to fresh country air and spectacular views.

FLOORS

The primary purpose of floors is a functional and structural one. Obviously they will be subject to heavy foot traffic over years, probably decades, and should therefore be durable and reasonably easy to maintain. Such practical considerations cannot be ignored, but nor should the design potential of flooring be overlooked.

Floors can influence the microclimate of a room. A marble floor, for example, will become quite cold in a cool-climate area, particularly in a room that receives little or no sun, while a floor covered in soft carpet will never chill the air. Flooring can also affect the acoustics of a room. Soft surfaces tend to absorb sound, while hard surfaces, such as wood and stone, reflect it. A change in flooring can be used to define different areas in a large open-plan area, achieving a visually comforting sense of order while maintaining the generous proportions of

A combination of light and dark woods packs a huge decorative punch at little more cost than the installation of a single type of wood.

a space without dividing walls. These are just three examples of the way in which flooring can make the difference between a space that is cold, loud and chaotic and one that is warm, intimate and orderly.

And, of course, flooring can play a role in establishing the decorative tone of a room, from the rustic roughness of sea-grass matting to the old-world glamour of parquetry or the minimalist chic of polished concrete.

The choice of flooring material is almost as important as the design of the floorplan itself. Indeed, while certain materials have a naturally limited lifespan, it is possible that the flooring you select will last as long as the house stands, influencing for generations the character of every room and the uses to which it is put.

Twelve-inch (30-cm) ceramic tiles emphasize the broad dimensions of this galley kitchen. They show their versatility, too, extending into both the formal living and dining areas and the casual, family spaces at either end of an expansive open-plan room.

WOOD

Warm and organic, wooden floors have the capacity to read differently according to their context: grand and traditional in a period home, homely in a country cottage, elegant in a parquetry-floored apartment, funky in a warehouse conversion or softly timeworn in an old beach house.

Different species of woods offer different hues and grains, from the various types of rugged, knotty, honey-toned pine, through to the fine-grained dark brown of tallow wood or blackbutt hardwood. Buying plantation wood ensures that the floorboards have not been fashioned from a threatened species or sourced from rainforests.

Recycled or salvaged floorboards have been retrieved from demolished or refurbished buildings. They tend to have more character than new floorboards and sometimes come in extra-large widths that have been deemed infeasible to produce in modern mills. These can add charm to any room, but make a particularly sympathetic surface choice in a refurbished period home. The extra work involved in sourcing, removing, sorting and re-presenting recycled floorboards adds to their cost relative to brand-new floorboards.

Remilled floorboards are large, structural beams, such as roof beams, that have been milled into conventional tongue-and-groove form. The main advantage of these is that they can achieve unusually broad widths, up to 10 or 12 inches (25 or 30 cm) in some cases. Remilled floorboards are a rarer, more labor-intensive product and therefore tend to be even more expensive than recycled floorboards.

❶ Resilient wooden flooring has been used throughout the high-traffic areas of this family home. A switch is made to carpet in a reading room, where softer acoustics are appreciated.

❶

❷ The intricate construction of a parquetry floor makes it all the more susceptible to the warping and splitting problems to which wood is prone in hot or humid climates. Properly installed, it can be used in such areas as kitchens, but is probably best avoided where the environment is particularly demanding, for example in an ocean-front apartment. ❷

① The blond tone of maple flooring evokes the pale, pared-back character of Scandinavian interiors. The pure white walls and light-colored floor also serve as a dramatic contrast to striking artworks and eye-catching furniture.

①

Way down the scale in terms of price is the plywood floor. Plywood is made from layers of pine, with the grain of each consecutive layer laid at right angles to the one before it. This structure gives the material great stability. Plywood comes in different grades, the lowest and least expensive grade being composed of layers with many knots in the wood, while the highest and most expensive grades contain few knots. The top-of-the-range product is often called "marine-grade ply," and is commonly used as a building material on yachts. Plywood comes in sheet form and can be screwed onto joists to make an unusually low-cost wooden floor. The disadvantage of plywood is that its surface is just the upper layer of many, very thin veneers and can be damaged relatively easily.

Wood can be badly affected by water, so must be sealed. The most common and most practical sealants are synthetic finishes, such as polyurethane, and oil finishes. These are prone to scratches and will wear down over time, so they must be sanded back and reapplied every three or four years.

② A patterned, painted wooden floor camouflages the inevitable spills and splashes of the kitchen. It also makes a clear distinction between the workspace and the living areas of this open-plan room.

②

LINOLEUM

Linoleum has been the subject of some misconceptions over the last few decades. Often confused with vinyl, which is a synthetic material, linoleum is a natural product made from a mixture of ground cork, linseed oil, wood resins and wood flour, which is then pressed onto a natural-fiber backing. It also has a reputation for a tendency to crack and split, a failing that was true of linoleum floors in the first half of the 20th century, but not one to which the improved, modern product is prone. This natural and durable flooring material is also warm underfoot and acoustically gentle, a plus for anyone who despairs of the clattering echoes produced in rooms lined with hard surfaces. And it is a naturally antibacterial surface, hence its regular appearances in hospitals, where hygiene is a priority. Modern linoleum comes in hundreds of base colors. A range of decorative insets and border strips is also available. It can be laid in tiles or in sheet form, but special care must be taken during installation to ensure that moisture can't get in

❶ The use of stone flooring throughout both the indoor and outdoor areas of this unconventional house reinforces the notion that they are all part of the available living space. The polished stone of the living room floor extends right to the edge of a water feature that runs through the covered entry.

❷ Decorative insets and borders can be incorporated into almost any type of flooring, including stone, wood, linoleum and vinyl. Such embellishment adds to the expense, but guarantees a highly individual finish.

❸ The decision to use particle board for this floor left room in the budget for the purchase of high-quality surfaces and equipment.

under the surface; if it does, the natural-fiber backing will rot and the floor will have to be replaced. Linoleum is popular in kitchens, but its characteristics also make it a sound choice for family dining areas or playrooms.

CORK

Like linoleum, cork is an agreeably organic product that is soft and warm to the touch. Cork tiles are made by mixing granulated cork with either natural or synthetic binders, then baking them. Natural cork tiles usually have a chestnut tone, but they are also available bleached or tinted in a variety of pastel shades. The tiles are sealed in situ and should be sanded back and refinished every three or four years.

RUBBER

Rubber represents yet another natural product choice, being made from the sap of the rubber tree mixed with any of a number of bonding ingredients, including chalk, cork and powdered slate. Rubber comes in tile or sheet form and is available in an overwhelming array of colors. Studded rubber is a particularly good choice in the kitchen or bathroom, its nonslip surface proving valuable in wet areas. Rubber can also be a brilliantly colorful, soft surface option in playrooms.

Cork is a sensible choice in an open-plan living area, going some way to countering the noise problems that are often associated with large internal spaces.

VINYL

Vinyl, a synthetic material, has two great advantages. First, it is essentially a low-cost product, although some manufacturers produce a premium product with comparably higher prices. Secondly, it can be made to replicate just about every other flooring surface: wooden floorboards, bamboo, slate, marble, mosaic — the lot. This versatility makes it possible to replicate those looks in situations where the authentic material is either too expensive or too difficult to install. For example, vinyl could be laid over an existing floor in an apartment to give a sophisticated parquetry look without the associated expense, noise problems or rise in floor height. Regular sweeping and mopping will keep the surface in good order for years, another advantage over such materials as wood, which needs to be resurfaced every two or three years. Vinyl comes in both tile and sheet form.

❶

❷

CERAMIC TILES

Ceramic tiles are most commonly used in bathrooms and kitchens, but can also be installed in living areas, giving an appealingly casual, indoor–outdoor look that evokes the style of Mediterranean homes. The variation in price from the basic, square, single-color tile to the very top-of-the-range product is phenomenal. For use as a flooring surface, choose tiles with a matte glaze; those with a high-gloss finish are unsuitable for this purpose because they can be slippery when wet. Tiles will stand up to many decades of foot traffic, but if a heavy object is dropped onto the surface the tiles are very likely to crack or chip. Particularly well suited to floor installation are fully vitrified tiles. These have a matte finish and, unlike glazed tiles, are a solid color throughout, meaning that the small chips that start to appear after years of heavy use will not be glaringly obvious. Like all hard surfaces, tiles will reflect sound, which could result in a noisy room.

③

TERRA COTTA

Terra-cotta floors are composed of tiles of baked clay. They
have a warm and earthy look, but are extremely porous and
must be sealed for use inside the house. Some sealers darken
the color of the natural tile. Terra cotta tends to absorb and
retain heat and while this may be a bonus in cool climates, it
could contribute to a hot and stuffy interior in warmer climates.

MARBLE

Marble can be laid in tile or slab form. It is an inherently
cold material, though underfloor heating can be installed to
rectify that tendency. The color of marble ranges from whites
and pale grays through to roses and some quite dark greens,
all with the characteristic random veining. Marble is a porous
material and must be sealed to avoid stains.

① Polished concrete is one of those elements
that can adapt to various architectural styles.
Here it has the classic look of a stone floor,
yet it can also be used in cutting-edge
contemporary interiors.

② Interior tiles are often too delicate for
external use, but tiles produced for exterior
application can generally be used in internal
rooms to achieve an attractively casual,
indoor–outdoor feeling.

③ Opting for tinted concrete means being
able to specify precisely the hue of the floor.
Here, the floor has been expertly color-
matched to the feature wall.

GRANITE

Granite is another magnificent stone surface ranging in color from beige to rusty red to near black. It has a characteristic strength and resilience that will probably never be tested in a domestic interior. Like marble, it is a naturally cold material that may require underfloor heating in a cold climate. It is extremely heavy and should not be installed on floors that have an inadequate load-bearing capacity.

TERRAZZO

Terrazzo is a wonderful hybrid product that has something of the nature of a stone floor, but in a range of looks that embraces the warm, the classic, the whimsical and the cheeky. Terrazzo is made by strewing a decorative aggregate material, such as marble, shell, colored glass or metal fragments, through a concrete base. The aggregate can appear as seed-sized granules or pebble-sized chunks. The product can be customized further by adding tints to the concrete base. Terrazzo can be poured in situ or laid as slabs or tiles. It is similar in price to such natural stones as granite and marble, so the selection of terrazzo should be motivated by aesthetic considerations rather than budget.

CONCRETE

Concrete is a product that has been reborn as a design material in recent years. Raw concrete slab floors can be polished to a luminous, stylish and edgily sophisticated finish or overlaid with a tinted screed, then buffed and sealed. Giving a polished finish to a raw floor is a reasonably inexpensive treatment, but tinted screeds or those that incorporate decorative particles, terrazzo-style, can be more expensive. An existing floor can be painted with exterior-grade paint for a low-cost makeover. A concrete floor is naturally porous, so must be appropriately sealed.

CARPET

The various carpet products available represent an extraordinary range in terms of quality. Overall, those with a denser weave and a lower-cut pile tend to be more resilient than those with a loose weave and a tall pile. Wool carpets are highly desirable: they both feel luxurious and wear extremely well. Wool is, however, an expensive option. As a compromise, consider a wool–acrylic blend; such blends may not feel quite as plush, but they can look much the same as a pure wool carpet and do offer similar durability. Carpets must be treated with a stain inhibitor and should be vacuumed regularly to eliminate the particles of grit that can settle into the pile and wear away at individual fibers, causing the material to age prematurely.

NATURAL FIBERS

Natural-fiber floors have a more robust appearance than carpeted floors. The least expensive is coir, a fiber that usually appears in a fairly broad, chunky weave. It is tremendously durable and can be an excellent choice for stairs and hallways, but it is sensitive to humidity and may even attract mold. Slightly more refined is sisal, a fiber that can be produced in a fine and elegant weave. Weaves that incorporate intricate textures or complex colorways are broadening the appeal of sisal and turning it into a mainstream, decorative alternative to traditional carpeting. Sisal is anti-static, durable and easy to maintain but, like coir, is sensitive to moisture. Jute has a similar appearance to sisal and tends to be lower priced, but is markedly less durable. Sea-grass floors offer a smoother surface than those created with the more fibrous alternatives of sisal, coir or jute, yet they still could not be described as a soft surface. An advantage of sea grass is that it is naturally water-proof, so does not attract the moisture problems associated with those other natural-fiber floorings.

❸

❶ Terrazzo is a material that has many different personalities depending on its components. It can be quirky and garish, hard and industrial or soft-hued and subtle. Here, flecks of barley and pewter mirror the tones of the bathroom cabinetry.

❷ In a brand-new residence designed to look like a 17th-century farmhouse, soft-hued tiles are used to re-create an aged flagstone floor.

❸ In a sitting room of refined luxury and formal elegance, no type of flooring is more appropriate than plush carpet.

STAIRCASES AND HALLWAYS

Staircases and hallways are often accorded a low status in house planning. Certainly in most cases they do not present the decorative potential of a living area or fulfill the intensely functional purpose of a kitchen or a bathroom, yet they can be fundamental to the success of a house or apartment.

They are, of course, the means by which all other rooms are accessed and thus can have a huge impact on how livable the house is. If a passageway is too thin, too dark, too awkward or poorly oriented, then the extent to which the rooms within its reach are used may be adversely affected. Similarly, if the only route to an attic conversion is by a drop-down ladder, then the uses to which that space can be put — and by whom — are decidedly restricted.

Passageways are responsible for more than human traffic; they also aid the movement of light and air around the house. Nowhere is that role more apparent than in the early vernacular architecture of northern Australia, where encircling verandahs were used to provide access to every room in the house, replacing internal corridors entirely, a ploy that reduced building costs. This external corridor also shaded all external windows and surrounded the structure with a belt of cooled air, achieving the most comfortable interior possible in a notoriously hot climate. Such pragmatic building practices might be less readily employed in modern homes, but the idea that halls and staircases might be utilized to promote ventilation and light penetration remains attractive.

❶ A mezzanine floor suspended from the ceiling makes the most of the available height in this narrow extension. The room is used only sporadically as a spare bedroom and occasional study, so a simple ladder can serve as access when required.

❶

❷ The sections of this corridor that border a courtyard have been lined with glass panels, which act as a source of natural light for both the hallway and the adjoining rooms.

❸ A masonry staircase clad with wood plays a decorative as well as a functional role. For safety reasons, some local authorities will not permit the construction of a staircase without a railing at the outer edge. Nonetheless, the effect is a structural component with strong graphic impact.

❹ A whitewashed staircase with stone insets imparts a strong Mediterranean feeling.

❺ Halls leave little room for functional furniture, but a feature piece can be used to confirm the character of the interior.

HALLWAYS

A standard hallway is not a place in which to linger. Long and thin, its primary purpose is to provide access to all the adjoining rooms. A hall, therefore, should never be cluttered with furniture: the slim dimensions of the space mean that almost any amount of furniture becomes an unsightly obtrusion, and is likely to hinder easy movement around the house. A slender table is acceptable, provided those using the hallway aren't obliged to squeeze past it as they make their way around. There's usually no room for an accompanying chair here, so the table will never be used for a functional purpose. Instead, use the tabletop to display a collection of favorite objects or an arrangement of photos. It's far better, however, to go without furniture altogether and think of your hallway as a gallery space, the walls hung with framed photographs or paintings.

❶ The double-height wall space of a staircase presents a fine opportunity for the display of art, especially when the landing is sufficiently wide to serve as a viewing platform.

❷ The owner of this house wanted to create spaces reminiscent of the colonnades of Venice. The house wraps around an internal courtyard with long walls of arched doors and windows facing onto halls and living spaces. As a result, the interior is always awash with light and filled with garden-fresh air.

❸ A slender hall table is a traditional inclusion in a period house. Use it as a display area for family photographs, small collectibles or fresh flowers, otherwise it may become a repository for all sorts of incidental clutter.

❶

Very few hallways incorporate external windows, so lighting — or the lack of it — is a key issue. Do what you can to stop the hall from becoming a dispiriting and dingy space. Keep away from dark paint colors unless you're committed to all the shadowy drama of an authentic period house, and look into the possibility of a skylight.

In a two-story house where light is a serious problem, consider using an unconventional flooring material in an upstairs hall as a means of bringing light through to lower levels. A floor of wooden battens, evenly spaced in the manner of an outdoor deck, is a clever solution that will allow light from second-floor windows or skylights to reach the lower floor. In a house with an industrial character, metal mesh or even toughened glass could be used in a similar way.

❶ In this house, a passageway required for access on an upper level realizes its full potential. The open construction ensures that the rooms upstairs benefit as much as possible from sources of natural light on the ground floor. Extra width allows just enough room for the walls of the hallway to be lined with bookshelves, forming an unorthodox but entirely useful family library.

❷

❷ Cutaways in the second-floor corridor bring light from rooftop skylights all the way down to the first floor.

❸ This glazed bridge links a late-Victorian cottage with its ultra-modern extension. The unusual construction signals the dramatic shift in architectural style, but also allows views of a Japanese-style pond below.

❹ Lined with louvers, this bridge functions to distance the main body of the house from an isolated main bedroom occupied by the parents of the family. The structure reinforces the notion of privacy and seclusion.

❸ ❹

STAIRCASES

Staircases are a high-traffic area and must be surfaced in a material that will stand up to considerable wear and tear. Wood does the job well and, if the staircase is made from a beautiful wood in the first place, its looks will actually improve with age as years of footfalls polish the surface and reveal a luminous grain. For safety's sake, treat the wood with a nonslip finish such as a matte varnish: a soft waxed surface could prove dangerous in this setting.

Stone and ceramic tiles are another alternative, although their excessive weight means that you will need a strong subfloor.

If you prefer something softer underfoot and want to carpet the staircase or install a runner, remember that the material must be tough enough to tolerate constant use. Be wary, though, of choosing a material that is overly thick or that has a particularly stiff backing: if it is too unyielding, you may have trouble bending it around the corners of the treads. A stain-retardant treatment is advisable, given that the shuffle of shoes, bare feet and paws will leave their mark over time.

Open staircases constructed from horizontal treads without the vertical risers are an excellent choice in confined spaces. They take up less room visually and permit airflow and light penetration that would otherwise be blocked by a bulky staircase. Spiral staircases can be used in even the most cramped situations, such as to provide access to an attic conversion. They can look very romantic and contribute real charm to a house, but remember that it can be nearly impossible to shift large pieces of furniture up those diminutive, twisting steps.

❶ This open staircase, comprising horizontal treads and no vertical risers, allows natural light, filtered through panels of polycarbonate sheeting on the exterior wall, to penetrate deep into the interior.

❶

❷ A spiral staircase is the most space-efficient way of moving between two levels.

❸ A sweeping staircase, designed with the grace that characterizes this magnificent home, is an undisputed showpiece.

❹ In this house, an open staircase was the most appropriate form of access to lead from a double-height, open-plan living area to the private rooms on the next level. It is visually lightweight and does not obstruct the flow of light and air around the interior.

❺ This house is a carefully considered hybrid of new and old building styles. The vaulted ceiling is a traditional form, but the open construction of the staircase complements the flowing living spaces of the modern house.

INDEX

CREDITS

1 Architect: John McGrail, Stewart Ross Team Architecture; Photographer: Doc Ross

2 Architect and interior designer: James Christou & Partners; Photographer: Robert Frith

4–5 Designer: Milvia Hannah, International Interiors; Photographer: Paul McCredie

6–7 Architect: Brian Zulaikha, Paul Rolfe and Rebecca Cleaves, Tonkin Zulaikha Architects; Photographer: Simon Kenny

8 (left) Designer: Glenn Holmes, Design Department; Photographer: Simon Kenny; (right) Image supplied by Textilia

9 Interior designer: Darryl Gordon Design; Photographer: Simon Kenny

10–11 Top row (left) Interior designer: Dana Lane, Candlewick; Photography: Shania Shegedyn; (center) Designer: Darren

Grayson; Photographer: Shania Shegedyn; (right) Architect: Shulze Poursoltan Architects; Photographer: David Sandison. Middle row (left) Designer: Lyn Orloff-Wilson; Photographer: Simon Kenny; (center) Architect: Julian Guthrie, Godward Guthrie Architecture; Photographer: Bruce Nicholson; (right) Architect: Mark Sheldon, GSA; Photographer: Simon Kenny. Bottom row (left) Image supplied by Century Furniture; (center) Designer: Suying Design; Photographer: Tim Nolan; (right) Image supplied by The Biggie Best Shop

12–13 Interior designer: Jo Baker; Photographer: Anton Curley

14–15 (1) Designer: Michael O'Brien, de Giulio Kitchen Design; Photographer: John Miller; (2) Architect: Simon Novak,

Novak & Middleton Architects; Photographer: Paul McCredie; (3) Architect: Mason & Wales; Photographer: Doc Ross

16–17 Designer: Stanley Morris; Photographer: Peter Mealin

18–19 (1) Interior designer: Ros Palmer, Ros Palmer Interiors; Photographer: Simon Kenny; (2) Architect: Arclinea Design Pty Ltd; Photographer: Simon Kenny; (3) Architect/Interior designer: Roger Walker Architects; Photographer: Paul McCredie

20–21 Architect: Andrew Patterson, Architects Patterson & Co; Photographer: Bruce Nicholson

22 Architect: Chan Soo Khian, Rene Tan, Stephany Weng, SCDA; Photographer: Peter Mealin

22–23 Interior designer: George Budiman; Photographer: Tim Nolan

24–25 (1) Interior designer: Abie Petraska, Ambiance Interiors; Photographer: Anton Curley; (2) Interior designer: Dean Sharpe and Neal McLachlan, Revolution Interiors; Photographer: Claude Lapeyre; (3) Architect: Guz Wilkinson Architects; Photographer: Luca Invernizzi Tettoni and Tim Nolan

26–27 (1) Architect: Edwin Elliot Architect; Photographer: Lloyd Park; (2) Design: Rocky Amatulli and Jenny Baron-Hay in conjunction with Craig Steere Architects; Interior designer: Baron-Hay & Associates; Photographer: Robert Frith

28–29 (1) Designer: Stanley Morris; Photographer: Peter Mealin; (2) Interior designer: James Young, Jacqueline & Associates; Photographer: Kallan MacLeod; (3) Designer: Cameron Kimber; Photographer: Simon Kenny; (4) Interior designer: Suzie Beirne, Maison Jardin; Architectural draftsman: Robin Payne; Photographer: David Sandison; (5) Architect and interior designer: Ben Trogdon, Ben Trogdon Architects; Photographer: Steve Keating

30–31 (1) Architect: Brian Cullen, Patterson, Cullen & Irwin; Photographer: Bruce Nicholson; (2) Interior designer: Thomas Hamel; Photographer: Simon Kenny; (3) Architect: Adam Mercer and Dick Mercer, Mercer & Mercer Architects; Photographer: Anton Curley

32 Image supplied by Firth Industries

32–33 Main contractor and developer: YTL Development; Photographer: Gérald Lopez

34–35 Peter Bromhead, Bromhead Design Associates; Photographer: Anton Curley

36–37 (1) Architects: Morehouse MacDonald and Associates; Photographer: Sam Gray; (2) Image supplied by Firth Masonry Villa; (3) Architect and interior designer: James Christou & Partners; Photographer: Robert Frith

38–39 (1) Interior designer: Jill Goatcher, Intext Design; Architect: Juan Molina Arquitectura; Photographer: Bruce Nicholson; (2) Architect: Chuck Peterson; Photographer: Tim Maloney; (3) Architect: Kerry Fyfe, Monckton Fyfe Architects; Photographer: Simon Kenny; (4) Architect and interior designer: James Christou & Partners; Photographer: Robert Frith

40–41 Architect: Brian Brand, Baylis Architects; Photographer: Steve Keating

42–43 (1) Interior designer: Sue Naylor, Naylor Booth Associates; Architectural designer: Crofton Umbers Design; Photographer: Anton Curley; (2) Designer: Jane Agnew; Photographer: Robert Frith; (3) Architect: David Luck, David Luck Architecture; Photographer: Shania Shegedyn; (4) Interior designer: Abie Petraska, Ambience Interiors; Photographer: Anton Curley; (5) Interior designer: Glasgow Architects, Robert Hanson and Maggie Bryson Interiors; (6) Architect: Glasgow Architects & Robert Hanson; Photographer: Kallan MacLeod

44–45 (1) Architect: Hulena Co Architects; Photographer: Kallan MacLeod; (2) Interior designer: James Young, Jacqueline & Associates; Photographer: Kallan MacLeod; (3) Architect: Simon Novak, Novak & Middleton Architects; Photographer: Paul McCredie

46–47 (1) Architect: James Cioffi; Photographer: Tim Maloney; (2) Architect: John Blair, Blair + Co; Photographer: Doc Ross; (3) Image supplied by Eden Homes; (4) Designer: Peter Bromhead, Bromhead Design Associates; Photographer: Anton Curley

48–49 (1) Interior designer: Talla Skogmo, Gunkelman Interior Design; Architect: Kelly Davis, SALA Architects; Photographer: Tim Maloney; (2) Interior designer: Cathy Cowell, Cathy Cowell Designs; Photographer: David Sandison

50–51 Designer: Garth Barnett Design; Photographer: Simon Kenny

52–53 (1) Interior designer: Shami Griffin; Architect: Fery Poursoltan, Schulze Poursoltan Architects; Photographer: Gérald Lopez; (2) Architect: Kerry Mason, Architecture Warren & Mahoney; Photographer: Lloyd Park

54–55 (1) Architect: Darren Jessop, Jessop Townsend Architects; Photographer: Bruce Nicholson; (2) Architect: Craig Craig Moller; Photographer: Bruce Nicholson; (3) Designer: Robyn Labb, Kitchens by Design; Photographer: Bruce Nicholson

56–57 (1) Architect: Gary O'Reilly, Architectural Projects; Photographer: Simon Kenny; (2) Designer: Graheme McIntosh; Photographer: Simon Kenny; (3) Architect: Simon Carnachan, Carnachan Architects; Photographer: Bruce Nicholson

58–59 (1) Image supplied by Peter Fell; (2 & 3) Designer: Walter Herman, Ros Palmer Interiors; Photographer: Simon Kenny

60–61 (1) Architect: John Blair, Blair + Co; Photographer: Doc Ross; (2) Architect: Morrison Architects; Photographer: Randy Foulds

62 Architect: Mark Fosner and Bruce Fabrick, Moon Bros; Photographer: John Umberger

62–63 Architect: Craig Craig Moller; Photographer: Bruce Nicholson

64–65 (1) Kitchen designer: Shirley McFarlane, Kitchensmith; Photographer: Thomas Birdwell; (2) Architect: John Mills Architects; Builder/Kitchen manufacturer: MB Brown; Photographer: Paul McCredie; (3) Interior design: Jackson Clements Burrows and Cardamone Design; Architects: Jackson Clements Burrows; Photographer: Shania Shegedyn

66–67 (1) Interior designer: Abie Petraska, Ambience Interiors; Photographer: Anton Curley; (2) Architect: Chris Wilson, Wilson & Hill Architects; Photographer: Lloyd Park; (3) Designer: Sandra Grummitt; Photographer: Anton Curley; (4) Designer: Sandra Grummitt; Photographer: Anton Curley; (5) Designer: Chris Ralston; Photographer: Anton Curley

68–69 (1) Architect: Paul Clarke, Crosson Clarke Architects; Photographer: Bruce Nicholson; (2) Architect: Sarah Shand; Photographer: Anton Curley; (3) Kitchen designer and manufacturer: Jos van Bree, Domus Kitchens; Photographer: Peter Hyatt

70–71 Designer: Chris Ralston; Photographer: Anton Curley

72–73 (1) Architect: Sam Wells and Diana L. Marley, Sam Wells and Associates; Photographer: Tim Maloney; (2) Architect: Karl Romandi, Karl Romandi & Helen DeLuis Architects; Photographer: Simon Kenny; (3) Architect: Sam Wells and Diana L. Marley, Sam Wells and Associates; Photographer: Tim Maloney

74–75 (1) Architect: Brian Quirk, Quirk & Albakri; Photographer: Peter Mealin; (2) Architect: Brian Quirk, Quirk & Albakri; Photographer: Peter Mealin; (3) Designer: Leon House, Leon House Design; Photographer: Robert Frith

76–77 (1) Architect: Sheppard & Rout; Photographer: Lloyd Park; (2) Designer: Cameron Kimber; Photographer: Simon Kenny; (3) Designer and manufacturer: John Horvath, Hardy Interiors, Furniture and Kitchens; Photographer: Simon Kenny; (4) Architect: Richard Priest Architects; Photographer: Anton Curley; (5) Kitchen Designer: Clive Champion; Photographer: Shania Shegedyn

78–79 (1) Architect: Kerry Mason, Architecture Warren & Mahoney; Photographer: Lloyd Park; (2) Designer: Milvia Hannah, International Interiors; Photographer: Paul McCredie; (3) Kitchen Designer: Veryan Del Moro, Italy and Kitchens; Photographer: Anton Curley; (4) Designer: Michael O'Brien, de Giulio Kitchen Design; Photographer: John Miller

80–81 Designer: Sue Gillbanks; Photographer: Anton Curley

82–83 (1) Architect: Paul Clarke, Crosson Clarke Architects; Photographer: Bruce Nicholson; (2) Architect: Darren Jessop, Jessop Townsend Architects; Photographer: Bruce Nicholson; (3) Designer: Creazioni Kitchens; Photographer: Anton Curley

84–85 (1) Kitchen Design: Sally Holland and Tony Parker; Photographer: Anton Curley; (2) Architect: Gerard Murtagh; Photographer: David Sandison; (3) Kitchen designer: Paolo Cozzolino, Creazioni Kitchens and Shami Griffen; Photographer: Gérald Lopez; (4) Image supplied by Julius Blum

86–87 (1) Kitchen design: Paolo Cozzolino, Creazioni Kitchens and Shami Griffen; Photographer: Gérald Lopez; (2) Image supplied by Henry Brown Kitchens

88–89 (1) Architect: Athfield Architects; Photographer: Paul McCredie; (2) Karl Romandi, Karl Romandi & Helen DeLuis Architects; Photographer: Simon Kenny; (3) Interior designer: Anne Tallot; Architectural consultant; Kim Veltman, Architectural Consultants; Image supplied by Fisher & Paykel; (4) Architect: Grant Amon; Photographer: Shania Shegedyn

90 Interior designer: Joey and Chris Makalinao, McLinao Design Studio; Architect: Chan Sau Yan Associates; Photographer: Peter Mealin

90–91 Architect; Leo van Veenendaal; Photographer: Anton Curley

92–93 (1) Architect: Sang Architects & Company; Photographer: Kallan MacLeod; (2) Designer: Maggie Bryson; Photographer: Anton Curley; (3) Interior designer and art consultant: Lenore West; Architect: Pat Jeffares; Photographer: Kallan MacLeod; (4) Architect: Lindy Leuschke, Leuschke Group Architects; Photographer: Bruce Nicholson; (5) Architect: Robert Harrington and Associates; Photographer: Simon Kenny

94–95 (1) Architect: Shelly Gane, Cook Sargisson & Pirie; Photographer: Bruce Nicholson; (2) Interior designer: Selina Tay, Collective Designs; Photographer: Peter Mealin

96–97 (1) Designer: Fay Bresolin; Photographer: Paul McCredie; (2) Image supplied by Bos Design; (3) Architect: DTC Architects; Photographer: Peter Mealin

98–99 (1) Interior designer: Talla Skogmo, Gunkelman Interior Design; Architect: Kelly Davis, SALA Architects; Photographer: Tim Maloney; (2) Architect: Simon Novak, Novak & Middleton Architects; Photographer: Paul McCredie; (3) Architect: BBP Architects; Photographer: Shania Shegedyn

100–101 (1) Architect: Chuck Peterson; Photographer: Tim Maloney; (2) Designer: Jennie Dunlop, Dunlop Design; Photographer: Bruce Nicholson

102–103 (1) Architect: Giles Tribe Architects; Photographer: Simon Kenny; (2) Architect: Glasgow Architects & Robert Hanson; Photographer: Kallan MacLeod; (3) Designer: Chris Ralston; Photographer: Anton Curley

104–105 (1) Interior designers: Joey & Chris Makalinao, McLinao Design Studio; Architect: Chan Sau Yan Associates; Photographer: Peter Mealin; (2) Architect: Lawrence Sumich, Sumich Architects; Photographer: Bruce Nicholson

106–107 (1) Architect: Mark Fosner and Bruce Fabrick, Moon Bros; Photographer: John Umberger; (2) Architect: Kerry Mason, Architecture Warren and Mahoney; Project team: Stuart Paterson, Huia Reniti; Photographer: Lloyd Park

108–109 (1) Architect: Gerard Lynch, Kevin Hayes Architects; Photographer: David Sandison; (2) Architect: Simon Carnachan, Carnachan Architects; Photographer: Bruce Nicholson

110–111 (1) Interior Design: Darryl Gordon Design; Photographer: Simon Kenny; (2) Image supplied by Coronado Paint; (3) Architect: Jennifer Hill, Architectural Projects; Photographer: Simon Kenny

112–113 (1) Designer: Suying Design; Photographer: Tim Nolan; (2) Architect: Morehouse MacDonald and Associates; Photographer: Sam Gray; (3) Architect: Craig Craig Moller; Photographer: Bruce Nicholson; (4) Architect: Mason & Wales; Photographer: Doc Ross; (5) Architect: Brian Zulaikha, Paul Rolfe and Rebecca Cleaves, Tonkin Zulaikha Architects; Photographer: Simon Kenny

114 Architect: Jim Peoples, Johnson & Peoples Architects; Photographer: Gil Stose

114–115 Interior designer: Darryl Gordon Design; Photographer: Simon Kenny

116–117 (1) Architect/interior: Chan Soo Khain of SDCA Associates; Photographer: Peter Mealin and Tim Nolan; (2) Interior designer: Darryl Gordon Design; Project architect: James Roberts; Photographer: Simon Kenny

118–119 (1) Architect: Greg Warner, Walker Warner Architects; Photographer: Tim Maloney; (2) Architect: Treff LaFleche, LDA Architects; Photographer: Sam Gray; (3) Designer: Kareen Goode, Margaret Goode; Photographer: Steven Perry

120–121 (1) Image supplied by The Elegant Bathroom Design Company; (2) Architect: Victoria Hamer Architects; Photographer: Shania Shegedyn

122–123 (1) Interior designer: Mason Cowle, Suzie Wiley, Planit Architecture & Management; Photographer: David Sandison; (2) Architect: Lionel Morrison, Morrison Seifert Murphy; Photographer: Tim Maloney

124–125 (1) Architect: Robert Weir, Weir & Phillips Architects; Photographer: David Sandison; (2) Architect: Gary O'Reilly and Jennifer Hill, Architectural Projects; Photographer: Simon Kenny; (3) Image supplied by The Ondine Electronic Shower System

126–127 Interior designer; Dave Strachan; Architect: Pat de Pont; Photographer: Kim Christensen

128–129 (1) Heather Menzies; (2) Designer: Glenn Holmes, Design Department; Photographer: Simon Kenny

130–131 (1) Image supplied by Imperial Home Décor Group; (2) Architect: Bill Harrison and Rick Hatch, Harrison Design Associates; Photographer: John Umberger

132–133 (1) Architect: Peter Ho, Graphoz Design; Photographer: Tim Nolan; (2) Interior designer: Thomas Hamel; Photographer: Simon Kenny

134–135 (1) Heather Menzies; (2) Architect: Scott Phillips and Peggy Deamer, Deamer & Phillips Architects; Photographer: Jonathan Wallen

136–137 (1) Interior designer: Carol Hyland; Architect: Fery Poursoltan, Schulze Poursoltan Architects; Photographer: Anton Curley; (2) Architect: Tigerman

McCurry Architects; Photographer: Leslie Schwartz

138–139 (1) Architect: Peter Lee, JPL Architectural Partnership; Photographer: Peter Mealin; (2) Architect: Pavlo Szyjan; Photographer: Robert Frith; (3) Architect: Gregory Maire; Photographer: Mike Kaskell

140–141 (3) Interior designer: James Young, Jacqueline & Associates; Photographer: Kallan MacLeod; (2) Architect/Interior designer: Andrew Nimmo, Annabel Lahz, Lahz & Nimmo Architects; Photographer: Brett Boardman; (3) Architect: Kerry Fyfe, Monckton Fyfe Architecture; Photographer: Simon Kenny

142–143 (1) Heather Menzies; (2) Designer: Christine Julian, Julian Kitchen Design; Photographer: Mike Kaskell

144–145 (1) Architect: John Blair, Blair + Co; Photographer: Doc Ross; (2 & 3) Architect: Graham Pitts; Photographer: Bruce Nicholson

146–147 (1) Designer: Christine Julian, Julian Kitchen Design; Photographer: Mike Kaskell; (2) Architect/Interior designer: Andrew Nimmo, Annabel Lahz, Lahz & Nimmo Architects; Photographer: Brett Boardman

148–149 (1 & 2) Architect: Brian Brand, Baylis Architects; Photographer: Steve Keating

150–151 (1 & 2) Designer: Cheng Design; Photographer: Tim Maloney; (3) Interior designer: Shami Griffin; Architect: Fery Poursoltan, Schulze Poursoltan Architects; Photographer: Gérald Lopez

152–153 (1) Architect: Steven Hensel, Hensel Design Studios; Photographer: Steve Keating; (2) Architect: Florian Architects; Photographer: Mike Kaskell

154–155 Architectural and interior design: Geoff Hardy; Photographer: Simon Kenny

156–157 (1) Architect: Gabriel Poole, Gabriel & Elizabeth Poole Design Company; Photographer: David Sandison; (2) Interior design: Arclinea Design; Photographer: Simon Kenny

158–159 (1, 2 & 3) Designer: Cameron Kimber; Photographer: Simon Kenny

160–161 (1) Architect: Kerry Mason, Architecture Warren and Mahoney; Project team: Stuart Paterson, Huia Reniti; Photographer: Lloyd Park; (2) Interior designer: Kirsti Simpson, Bligh Voller Nield Architects; Photographer: David Sandison

162–163 (1) Designer: Garth Barnett Design; Photographer: Simon Kenny; (2) Designer: Glenn Holmes, Design Department; Photographer: Simon Kenny; (3) Architect: Paul Uhlmann, Paul Uhlmann Architects; Photographer: David Sandison

164–165 (1) Designer: George Budiman, Cynosure Design; Photographer: Tim Nolan; (2) Interior designer: Talla Skogmo, Gunkelman Interior designer; Architect: Kelly Davis, SALA Architects; Photographer: Tim Maloney; (3) Architect: Robert Weir, Weir & Phillips Architects; Photographer: David Sandison

166–167 (1) Stylist: Louise Owens; Photographer: Simon Kenny; (2) Interior Design: Dana Lane, Candlewick; Photographer: Shania Shegedyn; (3) Interior designer: Shami Griffin; Architect: Fery Poursoltan, Schulze Poursoltan Architects; Photographer: Gérald Lopez

168–169 (1) Architect: Gerard Lynch, Kevin Hayes Architects; Photographer: David Sandison; (2) Architect: Glasgow Architects & Robert Hanson; Photographer: Kallan MacLeod; (3) Architect: Lindy Leuschke, Leuschke Group Architects; Photographer: Bruce Nicholson; (4) Architect: Jane Sachs and Thomas Hut, Hut Sachs Studio; Photographer: John Umberger

170–171 Designer: Isabelle Miaja, IMA Interiors; Photographer: Peter Mealin

172–173 (1) Architect: SCDA; Photographer: Peter Mealin; (2) Architect: Gabriel Poole, Gabriel & Elizabeth Poole Design Company; Photographer: David Sandison; (3) Image supplied by Firth Masonry Villas

174–175 (1) Image supplied by California Closets; (2) Interior designer: Roseneath Consultants; Architect: John Constable, Constable Hurst Architects; Photographer:

Anton Curley; (3) Design and contract supervision: James Valentine, Duncan Dempsey and Shaun Peyman, Inscape Design; Photographer: Paul McCredie

176–177 (1) Interior designer: Abie Petraska, Ambiance Interiors; Photographer: Anton Curley; (2) Architect: Eric Morrison and Pamela Rodriguez Morrison, Morrison Architects; Photographer: Mike Kaskell; (3) Main contractor and developer: YTL Development; Photographer: Gérald Lopez

178–179 Interior designer: Elaine Roberts – Homeworks; Architect: Brent Hulena and Michael O'Gorman, Hulena Architects; Photographer: Anton Curley

180–181 (1) Architect: Gabriel Poole, Gabriel & Elizabeth Poole Design Company; Photographer: David Sandison; (2) Architect: Warren Hedgpeth, Hedgpeth Architects; Photographer: Tim Maloney

182–183 Designer: Maggie Bryson; Photographer: Anton Curley

184–185 (1) Architect: Baylis Architects; Photographer: Steve Keating; (2) Image supplied by Cavit & Co; (3) Image supplied by Sleepyhead Manufacturing

186–187 (1) Interior designer and art consultant: Lenore West; Architect: Pat Jeffares; Photographer: Kallan MacLeod; (2) Interior designer: Anne Tallott; Architectural consultant: Kim Veltman Architectural Consultants; Photographer: Image supplied by Winstone Wallboards; (3) Image supplied by Textilia

188–189 Designer: Nigel Marshall, Marshall – The Home Creators; Interior designer: Sally Holland; Photographer: Anton Curley

190–191 Interior designer: Margot Cordony; Photographer: Simon Kenny

192 Interior designer: Sue Naylor, Naylor Booth Associates; Architectural design: Crofton Umbers Design; Photographer: Anton Curley

192–193 Architect/Interior designer: Roger Walker Architects; Photographer: Paul McCredie

194–195 Architect: Dale Mulfinger and Tim Fuller, SALA Architects; Photographer: Tim Maloney

196–197 (1) Image supplied by California Closets; (2) Architect: Robert Weir, Weir & Phillips Architects; Photographer: David Sandison

198–199 (1) Image supplied by California Closets; (2) Architect: Tim R. Bjella, Arteriors Architecture; Photographer: Tim Maloney; (3) Image supplied by Taubmans

200–201 (1) Interior design: Issenbel.com and Jillian Friedlander; Architect: Sarah Shand, Issenbel.com; Photographer: Kallan MacLeod; (2) Architect: Wilson & Hill Architects; Photographer: Doc Ross; (3) Interior design: Mark Broadley; Architect: Mark Broadley, Giles Tribe Architects; Photographer: Simon Kenny

202–203 (1) Architect: Darren Jessop, Jessop Townsend Architects; Photographer: Anton Curley; (2) Architect: Morehouse MacDonald and Associates; Photographer: Sam Gray

204–205 (1) Interior architect: Mauricio Gonzalez; photographer: Tim Nolan; (2) Interior design: Selina Tay, Collective Designs; Photographer: Peter Mealin

206 Architect: Ron Sang, Fairhead and Sang Architects; Photographer: Anton Curley

206–207 House, pool and landscape architect: Fery Poursoltan, Schulze Poursoltan Architects; Soft landscaping: Donald Gifford; Photographer: Anton Curley

208–209 (1) Architect: Peter Ho, Graphoz Design; Photographer: Tim Nolan; (2) Image supplied by James Hardie Building Products; (3) Architect: Robert Railley, Swan Railley Architects; Pool designer: Linda Clapham; Soft landscape designer: Mark Read, Natural Habitats; Photographer: Gil Hanly; (4) Landscape designer: Gary Boyle; Photographer: Bruce Nicholson; (5) Landscape designer: Trudy Crerar, Natural Habitats; Photographer: Bruce Nicholson

210–211 (1) Garden designer: Ted Smythe; Photographer: Bruce Nicholson; (2) Architect: Simon Youngleson;

Landscape architect: Boffa Miskell; Photographer: Lloyd Park; (3) Landscape designer: Darryl Mappin Garden Design Group; Photographer: David Sandison

212–213 (1) Landscape designer: Jamie Durie, Patio Landscape Design; Photographer: Simon Kenny; (2) Landscape architect: Ben McMaster, Inside Out Design; Photographer: Lloyd Park

214–215 (1) Landscape designer: Trudy Crerar, Natural Habitats; Photographer: Bruce Nicholson; (2) Architect: John Blair, Blair + Co; Photographer: Doc Ross; (3) Interior designer: Suzie Beirne, Maison Jardin; Architectural draftsman: Robin Payne Photographer: David Sandison; (4) Architect: John Blair, Blair + Co; Photographer: Doc Ross

216–217 (1) Architect: Gabriel Poole, Gabriel & Elizabeth Poole Design Company; Photographer: David Sandison; (2) Designer: Maggie Bryson; Photographer: Anton Curley; (3) Designer: Andrew Wiley; Photographer: David Sandison

218–219 (1) Landscape designer: George Budiman; Photographer: Tim Nolan; (2) Architect: Hulena Co Architects; Photographer: Kallan MacLeod; (3) Architect: John McGrail, Stewart Ross Team Architecture; Photographer: Doc Ross; (4) Designer: Jane Agnew; Photographer: Robert Frith

220–221 (1) Architect: Gerard Lynch, Kevin Hayes Architects; Photographer: David Sandison; (2) Architect: Robert Harrington and Associates; Landscape consultant: Adam Linton, Landscapes by Linton; Photographer: Simon Kenny

222–223 (1) Architect: Arclinea Design Pty Ltd; Photographer: Simon Kenny; (2) Interior and landscape designer: George Budiman; Photographer: Tim Nolan

224–225 (1) Architect: Chan Sau Yan Associates; Landscape architect: Michael White; Photographer: Peter Mealin; (2) Designer: Jane Agnew; Photographer: Robert Frith; (3) Architect: Pavlo Szyjan; Landscaping: Leo Collins; (4) Garden designer: Imperial Gardens Landscape;

Photographer: Leigh Clapp; (5) Architect: John McGrail, Stewart Ross Team Architecture; Photographer: Doc Ross

226–227 (1) Architect: Andrew Patterson, Architects Patterson & Co; Photographer: Bruce Nicholson; (2) Landscape designer: Tony Ward; Architect: Michael Suttor Architects; Photographer: Simon Kenny; (3) Landscape Architect: Mark Read, Natural Habitats; Photographer: Anton Curley

228–229 (1) Landscape designer: Jamie Loft, Out from the Blue; Photographer: Shania Shegedyn; (2) Landscape design consultant: Made Wijaya, Wijaya Landscape; Design architect: Sonny Chan, Chan San Yan Associates; Photographer: Peter Mealin

230–231 (1) Landscaper designer: Natural Habitats; Photographer: Anton Curley; (2) Interior designer: Abie Petraska, Ambiance Interiors; Photographer: Anton Curley; (3) Landscape designer: Ben McMaster, Inside Out Design; Photographer: Lloyd Park

232–233 (1) Architect: Paul Jones, Jones Coulter Young; Photographer: Robert Frith; (2) Landscape designer: Rick Eckersley, Eckersley Stafford Design; Photographer: Shania Shegedyn

234–235 (1) Design team: PT Wijaya Tribwana International, Made Wijaya, Michael White, design principal and Ground Kent Architects, Martin Grounds and Jack Kent design principal; Photographer: Gil Hanly; (2) Design architect: Sonny Chan, Chan San Yan Associates; Landscape design consultants: Joey and Chris Makalinao, McLinao Design Studio; Photographer: Peter Mealin; (3) Designer: Made Wijaya; Photographer: Gil Hanly

236–237 (1) Architect: Paul Uhlmann, Paul Uhlmann Architects, in association with Lisa Stone; Photographer: David Sandison; (2) Architect: Gabriel Poole, Gabriel & Elizabeth Poole Design Company; Photographer: David Sandison; (3) Architect: Pavlo Szyjan; Landscaping: Leo Collins; Photographer: Robert Frith

238–239 (1) Architect: Robert Harrington and Associates; Landscape consultant:

Adam Linton, Landscapes by Linton; Photographer: Simon Kenny; (2) Pool and landscape design: John Helyer and Martin Contractors Ltd; Photographer: Claude Lapeyre; (3) Landscape Designer: Trudy Crerar, Natural Habitats; Photographer: Bruce Nicholson

240–241 (1) Landscape designer: Jamie Loft, Out from the Blue; Photographer: Shania Shegedyn; (2) Architect: Chan San Yan Associates; Landscape architect: Michael White; Photographer: Peter Mealin

242–243 (1) Landscape designer: Ben McMaster, Inside Out Design; Photographer: Lloyd Park; (2) Landscape designer: Darryl Mappin; Photographer: Leigh Clapp; (3) Architect: Gabriel & Elizabeth Poole Design Company; Photographer: David Sandison; (4) Landscape designer: Jamie Durie, Patio Landscape Design

244–245 (1) Architect: Paul Jones, Jones Coulter Young; Photographer: Robert Frith; (2) Designer: Ben McMaster, Inside Out Design; Photographer Lloyd Park; (3) Architect: Simon Carnachan, Carnachan Architects; Photographer: Bruce Nicholson; (4) Architect: Ross Santa Maria, Impressions Pty Ltd; Photographer: Robert Frith

246–247 Landscape designer: Trudy Crerar, Natural Habitats; Architect: Andrew Patterson, Architects Patterson & Co; Photographer: Anton Curley

248–249 (1) Landscape architect: Robert Watson; Photographer: Gil Hanly; (2) Landscape designer: Jamie Durie, Patio Landscape Design; Photographer: Simon Kenny; (3) Landscape architect: Mark Read, Natural Habitats; Photographer: Anton Curley

250–251 (1) Landscape designer: Jamie Durie, Patio Landscape Design; Photographer: Simon Kenny; (2) Landscape designer: Darryl Mappin Garden Design Group; Photographer: David Sandison; (3) Landscape designer: Trudy Crerar, Natural Habitats; Photographer: Anton Curley

252–253 (left) Landscaping: Jamie Loft, Out from the Blue; Architect: Robert Blair

RAIA in association with McLauchlan & Associates Building Design Consultants, Melbourne; Photographer: Shania Shegedyn; (right) Architect: S2F; Photographer: Shania Shegedyn

254–255 (1 & 2) Landscape designer: Jamie Loft and Mira Martinazzo, Out from the Blue; Photographer: Shania Shegedyn; (3) Interior design: the owners; Architect: Leo van Veenendaal; Photographer: Anton Curley

256–257 (1) (left) all color panels: Photo Essentials; (second from left) Interior designer: Mary Durack, Mary Durack Interior Design; Architect: Geoffrey Pie, Geoffrey Pie Architect; Photographer: David Sandison; (center) Photo Essentials; (second from right) Interior designer: Mary Durack, Mary Durack Interior Design; Architect: Geoffrey Pie, Geoffrey Pie Architect; Photographer: David Sandison; (right) Photo Essentials. (2) (left) all color panels: Photo Essentials; Interior design: Jennifer Hill and client; Architect: Jennifer Hill, Architectural Projects; Photographer: Simon Kenny; (center) Photo Essentials; (second from right) Architect: Bud Brannigan; Photographer: David Sandison; (right) Photo Essentials. (3) (left) all color panels; Photo Essentials; (second from left) Image supplied by Bos Design; (center) Photo Essentials; (second from right) Architect: Ross Santa Maria, Impressions Pty Ltd; Photographer: Robert Frith; (right) Photo Essentials. (4) (left) all color panels: Photo Essentials; (second from left) Architect and interior designer: Geoff Hardy; Photographer: Simon Kenny; (center) Photo Essentials; (second from right) Designer: Veryan Del Moro, Italy and Kitchens; Photographer: Anton Curley; (right) Photo Essentials

258–259 Interior designer: Ray Lind, Martin Hughes Interior Architects; Photographer: Bruce Nicholson

260–261 (1) Architect: James McCalligan, JMA Architects; Photographer: Tim Maloney; (2) Architect: Warren Hedgpeth, Hedgpeth Architects; Photographer: Tim Maloney

262–263 (1) Image supplied by Coronado Paint; (2) Architect: Neil Cownie, Overman & Zuideveld; Photographer: Robert Frith; (3) Interior designer: Darryl Gordon, Darryl Gordon Design; Project architect: James Roberts; Photographer: Simon Kenny

264–265 (1) Architect: Simon O'Brien, Six Degrees Architects; Photographer: Shania Shegedyn; (2) Architect: Stewart Ross, Stewart Ross Team Architecture; Photographer: Doc Ross; (3) Architect: Gary O'Reilly, Architectural Projects; Photographer: Simon Kenny

266–267 Architect: John Mainwaring & Associates; Photographer: David Sandison

268–269 (1) Architect: Kerry Fyfe, Monckton Fyfe; Photographer: Simon Kenny; (2) Architect: Kerry Fyfe, Monckton Fyfe; Photographer: Simon Kenny; (3) Interior designer: Ray Lind, Martin Hughes Interior Architects; Photographer: Bruce Nicholson; (4) Designer: Glenn Holmes, Design Department; Photographer: Simon Kenny; (5) Architect: John Mills Architects; Photographer: Paul McCredie

270 Architect: Lindy Leuschke, Leuschke Group Architects; Photographer: Bruce Nicholson

270–271 Architect: Steve McCracken and Richard Archbold, Architecture Warren & Mahoney; Photographer: Anton Curley

272–273 Architect: Darren Jessop, Jessop Townsend Architects; Photographer: Bruce Nicholson

274–275 (1) Architect: Bud Brannigan; Photographer: David Sandison; (2) Architect: John Mills Architects; Project architect: Michael Melville; Photographer: Paul McCredie; (3) Architect: David L. Gray FAIA, David Lawrence Gray Architects; Photographer: Tim Maloney

276–277 (1) Architect: Tony Cardamone, Cardamone Design; Photographer: Shania Shegedyn; (2) Kitchen Designer: Mark White, CKD, Kitchen Encounters, assisted by Craig Heinrich; Photographer: Keel Harris

278–279 (1) Architect: Darren Jessop, Jessop Townsend Architects; Photographer: Bruce Nicholson; (2) Architect: Gabriel & Elizabeth Poole Design Company; Photographer: David Sandison

280–281 Architect: André Hodgskin Architects; Photographer: Anton Curley

282–283 (1) Image supplied by Alti New Zealand; (2) Landscape designer: Jamie Durie, Patio Landscape Design; Photographer: Simon Kenny; (3) Architect: John Mills Architects; Project architect: Michael Melville; Photographer: Paul McCredie

284–285 Architect: SCDA; Project team: Chan Soo Khian, Rene Tan, Stephany Weng; Photographer: Peter Mealin

286–287 (1) Architect: Victoria Hamer Architects; Photographer: Shania Shegedyn; (2) Architect: Julian Guthrie, Godward Guthrie Architecture; Photographer: Bruce Nicholson; (3) Architect: Sang Architects & Company; Photographer: Kallan MacLeod; (4) Architect: Jane Sachs and Thomas Hut, Hut Sachs Studio; Photographer: John Umberger

288–289 Designer: Vincent Interlandi Design Group; Photographer: Neil Lorrimer

290–291 Interior designer: Sharon Cross Interior Design; Photographer: Anton Curley

292–293 (1) Image supplied by Peter Fell Ltd; (2) Designer: Darryl Gordon Design; Photographer: Simon Kenny

294–295 (1) Architect: John Brooks; Photographer: Tim Maloney; (2) Architect: John Brooks; Interior designer: Abby Smith, Egan Design; Photographer: Tim Maloney

296–297 (1) Interior designer: George Budiman; Photographer: Tim Nolan; (2) Image supplied by Flooring Wholesale; (3) Architect: Michael Banney, m3architecture; Photographer: David Sandison

298–299 Designer: Clive Champion; Photographer: Shania Shegedyn

300–301 (1) Image supplied by Peter Fell; (2) Image supplied by The Slate and Stone Centre; (3) Image supplied by Peter Fell

302–303 (1) Architect: Interlandi Design Group Pty Ltd; Photographer: Shania Shegedyn; (2) Kitchen Design: Sally Holland and Tony Parker; Photographer: Anton Curley; (3) Designer: Glenn Holmes, Design Department; Photographer: Simon Kenny

304–305 (1) Architect: BBP Architects; Photographer: Shania Shegedyn; (2) Architect: Arclinea Design Pty Ltd; Photographer: Simon Kenny; (3) Architect: James McCalligan, JMA Architects; Photographer: Tim Maloney; (4) Image supplied by The Slate and Stone Centre; (5) Architect: Pat Jeffares; Photographer: Kallan MacLeod

306–307 (1) Designer: Stanley Morris; Photographer: Peter Mealin; (2) Architect: Dale Mulfinger and Tim Fuller, SALA Architects; Photographer: Tim Maloney; (3) Architectural design: Crofton Umbers Design; Photographer: Anton Curley

308–309 (1) Architect: Lindy Small, Lindy Small Architecture; Photographer: Tim Maloney; (2) Architect: Kerry Mason, Architecture Warren & Mahoney; Photographer: Lloyd Park; (3) Architect: Arclinea Design Pty Ltd; Photographer: Simon Kenny; (4) Architect: Paul Uhlmann, Paul Uhlmann Architects; Photographer: David Sandison

310–311 (1) Architect: Paul Uhlmann, Paul Uhlmann Architects, in association with Lisa Stone; Photographer: David Sandison; (2) Architect: Ross Santa Maria, Impressions Pty Ltd; Photographer: Robert Frith; (3) Architect: Frans Kamermans Architects Ltd; Photographer: Anton Curley; (4) Architect: Michael Hricak and Darrell S. Rockefeller, Rockefeller/Hricak Architects; Photographer: David Glomb; (5) Architect: Morehouse MacDonald and Associates; Photographer: Sam Gray

312–313 (1) Architect: Mark Fosner and Bruce Fabrick, Moon Bros; Photographer: John Umberger; (2) Architect: Wilson & Hill Architects; Photographer: Lloyd Park